MOE BERG

February 2 1975
with love from
Joseph
Harriet
and Edmund Guzjoe.

Louis Kaufman
Barbara Fitzgerald
Tom Sewell

MOE BERG

ATHLETE, SCHOLAR, SPY

Little, Brown and Company
Boston   Toronto

FIRST EDITION

To1/75

The authors are grateful to Dr. Samuel Berg for providing the photos used in this book.

The authors are grateful to the following companies for permission to reprint from previously published materials:
  The *Atlantic Monthly*, for the article "Pitchers and Catchers" by Moe Berg, as published in its September 1941 issue. Copyright 1941 by The Atlantic Monthly Company, Boston, Massachusetts.
  The Clarendon Press, Oxford, England, for excerpts from *Russian Grammar* by Nevill Forbes, Second Edition, 1916.
  The *Detroit News*, for an excerpt from H. G. Salinger's column "The Umpire," as published in the July 17, 1939 edition.
  WHDH Radio, for an excerpt from a column by Bill Cunningham, as published in the *Boston Herald*, February 26, 1942.

Library of Congress Cataloging in Publication Data

Kaufman, Louis, 1926–
  Moe Berg: athlete, scholar, spy.

  1. Berg, Moe, 1902–1972. 2. Baseball. I. Fitzgerald, Barbara, 1932– joint author. II. Sewell, Tom, joint author.
GV865.B38K38   1975   796.357'092'4 [B]   74-20540
ISBN 0-316-48348-6

Designed by Susan Windheim

Published simultaneously in Canada
by Little, Brown & Company (Canada) Limited
PRINTED IN THE UNITED STATES OF AMERICA

Dedicated to
Samuel Berg, M.D.

Acknowledgments

The authors are grateful to the more than two hundred persons who made this book possible.

From the ballplayers of the American and National leagues, to the scientists and military men on two continents involved in the race for the atomic bomb, to those who held secrets concerning Moe Berg and released them to honor the man, and to others who contributed in many important ways, we are particularly thankful.

Departments of the American government, including the Central Intelligence Agency, were sources of enlightenment, as were Michael Burke; H. K. Calvert; Joseph T. Cascarella; William Casey, chairman of the Export-Import Bank of the United States; Joseph Cronin, chairman of the American Baseball League; Dr. Antonio Ferri; George Gloss; Vernon "Lefty" Gomez; Professor Samuel Goudsmit; Professor Werner Heisenberg; John Kieran; Anita Loos; Mrs. Cecil Burton Lyon; Ted Lyons; Edward "Ted" Sanger; Al Schacht; Casey Stengel; Charlie Wagner; and Tom Yawkey.

We shall always remember approaching Dr. Samuel Berg at the Essex County Geriatrics Center in Belleville, New Jersey, asking for his assistance. He worked tirelessly from that moment and never retreated from sensitive interviewing.

Our sadness is that Arthur Daley of the *New York Times*, who contributed so movingly, died two weeks before the finish of the book. He had once considered writing this biography. Moe Berg was special to Arthur Daley and the reverse was also true.

May we toast some others who made writing this book a joy:

Professor Eduardo Amaldi, Elden Auker, Earl Averill, Warren S. Berg, Louis Berger, Marver Bernstein, Victor Borella, Robert Broeg, Dr. Lewis W. Brown, Asa Bushnell, former Navy Secretary John H. Chafee, Fred Cochran, Bob Considine, Crossan Cooper, Rita Coye, Daniel Coyle, Professor Luigi Crocco, William Crowley, Dan Daniels, Donald Davidson, Monsignor John Dillon Day, Marguerite DelGuidice, former Dartmouth College president John Dickey, Marlene Dietrich, Dominic DiMaggio, Otto Doering, Bill Doherty, Mrs. Barbara Doten, Mrs. Patti Ziegenhein Doten, Jay Dunn, former United States Postmaster James Farley, Mrs. Enrico Fermi, Americo Ferullo, Thomas Acton Fitzgerald, Reverend John Fogarty, Anne Ford, J. Russell Forgan, Professor William Fowler, Lillian Freitas, Professor O. R. Frisch, Robert Furman, William Geerhold, Charlie Gehringer, Harris Goldberg, Dan Golenpaul, June Gomez, Bill Grieve, Mrs. Leslie Groves, General Richard Groves, Dr. Milton Gustafson, Gelston Hardy, Dr. Hardy Hendron, Robert Holbrook, Jerome Holtzman, Lawrence Houston, Paul Hoye, Mrs. Edwin Hubble, Mrs. Pete Hurley, Cathy Ibbotson, Harold Kaese, Milton Kahn, Mrs. Morris Kaufman, Jim Kenny, Herbert Kenny, Mrs. John Kieran, Paul Kneeland, Diletta LaCortiglia, I. M. Levitt, Professor David Littlefield, Robert Liu, Harvard Dean George Lombard, Carrie Lutz, Cecil Burton Lyon, Pearl Lyons, Dr. Frank McCauley, S. Lang Makrauer, Earl Marchand, Mrs. Takizo Matsumoto, Mr. and Mrs. James G. Mullen, Jeremiah V. Murphy, Jerry Nason, Raymond Nelson, Norman Newhouse, John Ringling North, Suzanne Wiese Panciocco, Daisy Mae Patton, Eileen Peart, Harold Peters, Shirley Povich, Dave Powers, Marguerite Putnam, David Rahr, Michele Ricketts, Dr. Duncan Robertson, Russell G. Robinson, Larry Rosenthal, Sayre Ross, Edwin Rumill, Joseph Sabia, Professor Mario Salvadori, Dorothy Sewell, Luke Sewell, Jack Sharkey, Edna Shea, Daniel Sheehan, Ko Shioya, Arnold Silverman, Mrs. Carl Silverman, Red Smith, Professor Henry Smyth, Crocker Snow, Jr., David Sokolov, Mrs. Brenton Stevens, United States Senator Adlai Stevenson, III, Bill Stokinger, Bill Striker, Raymond Sutton, Sataro Suzuki, Alphonse "Tommy" Thomas, Peter Tompkins, Mrs. Harry Thompson, Professor Andrew J. Torrielli, Professor and Mrs. Hugh Townley, Judith Tropres, Felicia Value, Attorney Gerhard Van Arkel, Professor John Van Vleck, Professor Edward W. Wagner, Edward Weeks, Daniel White, John R. White, Dr. Gian Carlo Wick, Ted Williams, Sidney Yanes and Margot Zegarra.

Also, personnel of the Atomic Energy Commission, French, Italian, Japanese, Swedish and Swiss embassies, the

Diplomatic Branch of the National Archives, Princeton University, and the State Department.

Also, the files of: the *American Mercury, Atlanta Constitution, Boston Globe, Boston Herald, Boston Traveler, Chicago Tribune, Christian Science Monitor, Detroit News, Japanese Advertiser, New Orleans Times Picayune, New York Herald, New York Herald Tribune, New York Times, New York World-Telegram, Newark Evening News, Newark Ledger, Newark Star Eagle, Philadelphia Evening Bulletin, P.M., St. Louis Post-Dispatch, This Week Magazine, Trentonian, Washington Post,* and *Yomiuri Shimbun.*

Contents

MOE BERG

1
Japan

A LETTER FROM THE STATE DEPARTMENT of the United
States kept curious company among Moe Berg's catcher's
mitt, black kimono and medieval literature as the *Empress
of Japan*, bound for the Orient, sailed from British Van-
couver. The date was October 20, 1934. The letter, composed exactly two weeks earlier, read

To the American Diplomatic and Consular Officers:
　At the instance of the Honorable Chester C. Bolton, representative in the Congress of the United States from the State
of Ohio, I take pleasure in introducing to you Mr. Morris Berg
of Newark, New Jersey, who is about to proceed abroad.
　I cordially bespeak for Mr. Berg such courtesies and assistance as you may be able to render consistent with your official
duties.

　The letter was signed by Secretary of State Cordell Hull
under the administration of President Franklin Delano
Roosevelt.

Moe Berg boarded the *Empress* as a member of the United States baseball team, which had accepted an invitation from Japan to play its teams despite increasingly raw political relations between the two nations. Militarists in Japan were streaking toward expansionist adventures in China, the Pyrrhic victory at Pearl Harbor, and an atomic legacy.

The appearance of the American team, despite an enthusiastic reception that lay ahead, incited a cruel incident. Fanatic nationalists opposed the American team's presence and one zealot would plunge a sword into publisher Matsutoro Shoriki, the man most responsible for bringing the Americans to Japan.

The United States team was composed of players from the American League: Babe Ruth, who had just been given his release from the New York Yankees; Lou Gehrig and Vernon "Lefty" Gomez, also of the Yankees; Charlie Gehringer of the Detroit Tigers; Earl Averill, Clint Brown, and Berg of the Cleveland Indians; Jimmy Foxx, Eric McNair, Frank "Gabby" Hayes, Hal Warstler, Joe Cascarella, and Edmund J. Miller of the Philadelphia Athletics; and Earl Whitehill of the Washington Senators.

Also aboard the *Empress* was gentle Connie Mack, manager of the Philadelphia Athletics, who would direct the tour. Mack knew this was one of the most brilliant baseball teams ever assembled, a team immensely superior to the Japanese college teams it would encounter throughout the Empire.

Babe Ruth, the designated team captain, and Berg spent considerable time together aboard the *Empress*. The rugged catcher was among the home-run slugger's closest friends. Ruth trusted Berg and could confide in him. Berg returned that affection, admiring Ruth for his athletic ability and openness.

Moe was on his second trip to Japan. Two years earlier, in 1932, he, along with his friends pitcher Ted Lyons of the Chicago White Sox and Frank "Lefty" O'Doul of the Brooklyn Dodgers, who was then the batting champion of the National League, had been invited to Japan to coach its growing legions of baseball players. Although the game had become the national sport, the highest form of competition remained at the college level. But baseball proficiency was increasing and Japan dreamed of equality with America on the major league scale.

The arrival of the three athletes, in a Japan still exhilarated by its Manchurian victory of the previous year, triggered national attention. Despite the growing nationalism, the three Americans were revered for upgrading the playing caliber of hundreds of athletes at seven Tokyo universities. Berg showed the catchers the art of handling a pitcher, blocking home plate and his brilliant arm that gunned the ball to second base. Equally important, he spoke to the players in Japanese. Lyons, who was Moe Berg's closest friend in baseball, displayed the arm and the pitches that made him a legend — the change of pace, the sinker, the sneaky pick-off move. And the athletes marveled when O'Doul demonstrated hitting techniques that made him one of the greats of all time.

"Baseball fields were everywhere and the love of the game was incomparable," recalls Lyons. "And Moe combined his instruction with vigorous study of the Japanese language. He pursued it as if he were taking his doctorate.

The athletes were intrigued by his gifted linguistic ability and understood him perfectly. He was always probing ·them about the language. No matter where we went in Japan, Moe had a Japanese newspaper in his hand. He bought every paper in sight."

For Moe, the baseball demonstration was, in many ways, secondary. He had fallen in love with this mysterious nation: its beauty and history, the rhythm of its cities, the solitude of the countryside, the innate politeness of its people, the shyness of head-bowed women in the kimonos he loved, men gentle and curious. He found it strange that in the background a great antithesis prevailed and its intensity was growing.

"Moe never ceased to talk of Japan, the fascination was eternal," remembers Moe's brother, Dr. Samuel Berg, who as a major in the United States Army was destined to lead the first American medical team into Nagasaki after the atomic bomb.

The Japanese, in turn, found Moe a charming enigma. The combination of scholar-athlete elicited their traditional respect for accomplishment and newspapermen and photographers pursued him for interviews.

A 1923 graduate of Princeton, where he majored in Romance languages, earned high honors, and became its most noted baseball player, Berg began studying Japanese only months before leaving on the 1932 tour.

Professor Edward Wagner, chairman of the Department of East Asian Languages at Harvard University, said that, if Berg acquired knowledge of Japanese in the time reported, "it is utterly unbelievable, totally extraordinary and represents attainment that generally comes only after a great many years of study and living in Japan."

Sotaro Suzuki, then a newspaper reporter for *Yomiuri Shimbun*, now adviser to the Tokyo Giants, remembers:

"I met Moe Berg for the first time in 1932 when he came to Japan with Ted Lyons and Lefty O'Doul to coach baseball. This coaching of Japanese college boys contributed tremendously to their development toward modern major league baseball techniques. The three players were very popular, not only in the field, but in the towns.

"Moe became very quickly known to the Japanese people because he picked up the Japanese language very fast. He got along perfectly with the people because of his ability to speak Japanese, which is regarded as very difficult by Americans because of the difference in language construction. The Japanese regarded him as a multilinguist. Moe was respected as a fine, gentle and highly intelligent American by everybody who came in contact with him."

Suzuki recalls that Berg, besides demonstrating catching methods, was the "first baseball man" to teach Japanese players the techniques of hit-and-run plays and scoring after a fly ball to the outfield.

Suzuki noted in a column for *Yomiuri Shimbun* that Moe "studied under Professor Matsumoto of Meiji University" during the instructional period "and read through three volumes of the *National Reader*, a great feat indeed."

During this first visit, Kieo University in Tokyo asked Berg to join its faculty as professor of Romance languages. He was flattered by the offer and toyed with the idea, but baseball was his first priority and would remain so until World War II.

Now, in 1934, on his second Pacific crossing, Moe Berg never indicated that the trip was anything more than a

Moe Berg, carrying newspaper, aboard the *Asama Maru* upon arrival at Yokohama. Ted Lyons is at the rear. In front of Lyons is Lefty O'Doul.

Moe Berg explains the use of the hands in catching during an instructional session at Waseda University, Tokyo, in 1932.

Sotaro Suzuki, reporter for the Tokyo newspaper *Yomiuri Shimbun*, and Moe Berg, in 1932. Suzuki is now adviser to the Tokyo Giants.

Moe Berg, Frank "Lefty" O'Doul, Herb Hunter, and Ted Lyons in Tokyo, where they coached college baseball players in 1932. Hunter organized the tour.

Moe Berg explains a play at the plate to Japanese college players during the 1932 tour of Japan.

Moe, Ted Lyons, Lefty O'Doul, and Herb Hunter with Japanese movie stars.

American baseball instructors with Japanese students. Moe Berg is at top right with Ted Lyons. Seated in the center is Herb Hunter. Lefty O'Doul is seated third from right in a light gray suit.

baseball foray, and none of the surviving athletes years later could recall that it was. None of the ballplayers, however, had a State Department letter on the trip, and they expressed surprise that Moe Berg did.

The voyage was a happy one, with a stopover at Honolulu for an exhibition game. Most of the married athletes had brought their wives along and they and other women passengers chided Berg for remaining single. His standard response was that he would consider marriage "the year that I bat .300," an average that always eluded him. Berg remained a bachelor in a life that involved a number of beautiful women. Handsome in a dark, heavy-featured way, Moe Berg attracted women. In keeping with his penchant for privacy, Berg regarded his relationships with them as irrevocably personal, as was most of his life off the ball field. Babe Ruth's adopted daughter Julia, now Mrs. Brenton Stevens, who accompanied her parents to Japan, remembers "the trip was a graduation present and Dad, who was very fussy, never minded when I went out with Moe. It was really fun and exciting to be with him. There wasn't any subject he couldn't discuss and Moe was a gentleman with impeccable manners. Women of all ages were attracted to him. And he was a marvelous dancer. He was awfully good at the fox-trot and Lindy."

The trip across the Pacific was registered in record time despite rains and heavy seas. The *Empress* arrived at the Yokohama breakwater on November 2, and, as launches carried the Japanese press to the ship, the sun suddenly emerged. As soon as the photographers had climbed aboard, flashbulbs exploded around the American athletes, and Ruth laughed, saying, "I think I'm going blind." In reply to reporters' questions, Ruth said his future in baseball was uncertain, that he had received many offers to manage minor league teams but rejected them. He stressed what he said in the United States — that he would consider managing only in the major leagues.

Ruth continued: "I am sure the Japanese fans will see great pitching, sensational fielding and the most powerful hitting ever shown on the diamond anyplace in the world. And with this team, I am sure that we could beat any team in America."

Moe Berg served as interpreter for Ruth and Connie

Mack, who commented, "This trip to Japan has been eagerly anticipated by every member of the team. I am confident this trip will strengthen, further, the good relations between the United States and the Japanese Empire."

"Thank you Mr. Mack. Thank you Mr. Berg."

The wives of the ballplayers received floral bouquets at dockside from Miss Toshiko Onishi, the thirteen-year-old daughter of Yokohama Mayor Ichiro Onishi, and from Tayeko Furukawa, the fourteen-year-old daughter of Director S. Furukawa of the home bureau of the Kanagawa Prefectural Government. Mrs. Onishi headed a delegation of women who received the wives of the athletes.

The team arrived at Tokyo Station from Yokohama on a pleasant afternoon. No one was prepared for what lay ahead. Thousands of persons had descended on the station, and pandemonium broke out at the first glimpse of the athletes. They screamed "banzai" as they swarmed about the bewildered players.

"The density of the people was unbelievable," recalls Mrs. Stevens. "Many were waving American and Japanese flags. You would have thought the Emperor was among the people."

"Banzai Ruth" they screamed as they attempted to touch their hero.

"Banzai the great Gehrig."

"Banzai slugger Foxx."

"Banzai catcher Berg, the linguist."

"Gehringer of Detroit, banzai. Banzai Averill."

The ballplayers asked Berg to define "banzai" and he replied it was a tender Japanese greeting meaning "may you live ten thousand years."

Wives were lost in the struggle toward the waiting open

convertibles, which were to take them to the Imperial Palace to meet Emperor Hirohito and his Empress. When the Americans were finally inside their motorcars, the cortege was unable to move as thousands of workers leaving industrial plants created a massive jam. The police were powerless to control the crowd, which the Japanese press reported as exceeding one million persons in the eight-block Ginza district alone.

Streamers were hurled from office buildings and autograph seekers leaped on running boards with pieces of paper, school books, and parade banners to be signed.

Moe Berg signed his name in Japanese.

"I never saw so many people in my life," Gehringer recalls. "It was an unbelievable spectacle. One would have had to have seen it to appreciate its intensity."

Thousands of persons rushed ahead to Nijubashi Plaza, which abuts the Imperial Palace, to view the athletes entering sacred ground to meet Hirohito and his wife.

Cascarella, whom Berg admired during their baseball years as a bullpen ally, recollects:

"We were constantly being hosted by either a cabinet member or some part of the royal family. It went on every day, every night during the tour. Hirohito was in those days, you know, an untouchable. He was a god; you were not supposed to cast your eyes upon him. But when you were near the Emperor or royalty they evoked a solemnity and gentleness and a sense of grace.

"When we visited the palace, we were taken to a magnificent reception hall, and protocol dictated a subdued exchange of pleasantries, mostly characterized by standing and facing the Emperor.

"Suddenly during the formalities there was Moe Berg and the Emperor in conversation. I could see that the Emperor was enchanted by what Moe was saying. As Moe continued, a look of disbelief emerged on the traditionally stoic face of the Emperor — a disbelief that suggested wonderment that one of these baseball ruffians from a distant land could stand up to the son of god, use the language of the land, and have something vital to say.

"I'm not sure what was said, but I felt a sense of pride in Moe Berg. Where there may have been a deficiency in our behavior pattern, he helped heal the wounds."

"We were all in awe of Moe," remembers Mrs. Vernon Gomez. "It was a lovely reception given us by the Emperor and Empress. There was such a gentleness and politeness and a memorable majesty about it all. I remember mostly, I think, a great deal of polite bowing as is the Japanese custom. It was all very moving."

Leaving the palace the procession continued past city hall, where thousands of persons continued to shout their adoration and thousands of bicyclists made the traffic worse. The procession turned on the Shibaguchi and onto Tamuro-Cho to the Hibiya Amphitheater, where Japanese officials and thousands of baseball addicts were assembled for the official welcome to Japan.

Formally greeting the visitors were American Ambassador Joseph Clark Grew, who for many years, until his death, would send Christmas cards to Moe Berg; Tokyo Mayor Torataro Ushizuka, Eiji Amau of the Foreign Office, and Ryozo Hiranuma, president of the Tokyo University Baseball League.

It was sundown now and the crowd screamed for the

Babe to speak. The rotund hitter stood, and a deafening "banzai" hailed the world's most famous slugger. His emotion clearly visible, Ruth was terse. He waved and said: "We had come expecting a welcome from you but we did not expect the welcome to be of such magnitude. Speaking for the members of my party, may I say that each and every one of us will never forget, as long as we live, the warm reception you have given us. I thank you from the bottom of my heart. *Oyasumi Nasai*."

"Banzai Babe Ruth, banzai Babe Ruth."

The Babe turned to Berg, "Moe this has to be one of the greatest days of my life."

Japanese leaders and Ambassador Grew stressed the need for mutual understanding between nations and the furthering of world peace. They urged increased contacts between countries and suggested the appearance of the all-star team represented that philosophy.

The Toyama Military Band played "Stars and Stripes Forever." Then, with thousands standing in the bowl in a spirit of fellowship, the band played "Kimigayo," the Japanese national anthem, followed by the "Star-Spangled Banner."

"Banzai!"

The sixty-five thousand seats at Meiji Shrine had been sold out for the first game, and as the Americans emerged on the field for practice they were met by prolonged applause and banzais. The cheers for the home club, Tokyo, were equally robust.

Marquis Nobutsune Okuma, president of the newly formed Japan Baseball Club, who had never seen a baseball game in his life, began the pregame ceremony by throwing out the ceremonial first ball to Connie Mack. The throw was wild and Mack retrieved the ball near home plate, smiled, and handed the ball back to Okuma as a souvenir. Applause greeted the exchange.

Mack threw another ball to Earl Whitehill, the clever and temperamental left-hander of Washington, named to pitch the first game. Moe Berg was behind the plate.

The first batter for Tokyo, Masu, swung at the first pitch and hit it viciously past Whitehill into center field for a single. The crowd roared as if the hit were an omen of things to come, but the Tokyo first inning failed to produce a run.

America scored two runs in the first as Gehringer doubled to send McNair, who had walked, to third base. The anticipated roar for Ruth to hit a home run came, but starting pitcher Takshashi got Ruth to ground out and McNair crossed the plate. Lou Gehrig flied out to Masu and Gehringer scored after the catch.

Tokyo failed to score in the second. In the American half of the inning Moe Berg came to the plate and applause filled Meiji. Berg was hit on the left hip by the first pitch and the crowd gasped. Berg ran to first base unhurt and the crowd applauded vigorously. From the American dugout the ribbing commenced.

"Real vicious clout, Moe."

"Hey, tell those guys you haven't had a hit since Appomattox, Moe."

Berg turned toward the dugout and grinned.

Whitehill then hit cleanly to right and Berg raced to third, then scored on a single by McNair. The game ended with the Americans winning 17–1 as Whitehill scattered six hits through nine innings. Despite entreaties by the fans for home runs, none were hit.

Ruth was frustrated in his effort to hit a home run during the first four games. But in the fifth game, played in Tokyo, he hit his first home run in Asia, a drive into the right-field stands. When Ruth reached home plate, amid cheering that would last four minutes, he took off his cap and bowed in gratitude.

The game was won by the Americans 10–0, with Lefty Gomez striking out eighteen batters and allowing only two hits.

Formality accompanied the next day's game in Tokyo as teams of both nations stood along the first and third base foul lines to honor imperial visitors Prince Sumi, the youngest brother of the Emperor, Prince Kuninaga and Princess Michiko Kaya, who witnessed another American victory.

In mid-November Moe Berg was invited to speak to students at Meiji University in Tokyo. Jimmy Foxx and Lou Gehrig sat near Moe as he spoke from a stage.

He told the baseball-curious student body that America regarded Foxx and Gehrig as its two greatest active players. He characterized Connie Mack as a brilliant baseball tactician "and a kinder man and a better counselor I have yet to meet." Babe Ruth, Berg said, was the greatest single attraction in the history of sports, "absolutely in a class by himself."

Moe branched off from baseball to emphasize the need for closer relations between America and Japan. "I am particularly happy to be your guest again at Meiji University because of all that that great name brings up. It is particularly fitting for us to be here in our role of baseball players because I believe the Emperor Meiji, for whom your great university is named, would have been happy to see foreign commerce and intercourse spread to the world of sports. Those who know ever so little of Japanese history do know that it was during the prosperous era of Meiji that Japan bloomed into a world nation after Commodore Perry asked you to open your doors in 1853.

"And now added to your desire to trade with us and other nations you have done us the honor of adopting our national game as yours. There is no greater leveler, no greater teacher of humility than competitive sports. I sincerely hope that our innocent junket through Japan will serve to bring the countries whom we represent unofficially closer together. There is no better place than in the young heads of Meiji University students to think out ways and means of keeping our two countries in unison, fast and binding."

The students applauded Berg's talk, then presented him with a cigarette case. Thirty-eight years later Moe Berg still had it.

After the lecture and throughout the tour Moe met with Japanese scholars who sought advice on teaching English. In *American Mercury* magazine's May 1941 issue, a profile of Moe entitled "Dr. Berg, Backstop," written by David Brown and Ernest Lehman, noted that: "While he was with Connie Mack's all-star team on another trip to the Far East, Berg was able to deliver in that language the reply to the speech of welcome by a representative of the Japanese government. Before his departure from Japan on this latter trip, Moe lectured in one of the university classes and installed a system of English which is reported to be still in vogue. He made so favorable an impression, in fact, that he was invited to remain as instructor of languages at Kieo University. But Moe was not yet ready to give up baseball."

The games throughout the Empire were reported on the front pages of newspapers, and the Japanese became caught up in the hope of eventual victory over the Americans. The collegians were destined not to defeat the Americans during the sixteen-game tour, but several of the games were close.

An upset seemed possible in the game at Shizuoka as an eighteen-year-old Kyoto youth, Eiji Sawamura, battled Whitehill in a scoreless duel through six innings. Banzais soared through the stadium as Sawamura struck Ruth out the first two times he batted. In the seventh inning Lou Gehrig hit a Sawamura fast ball deep into the right-field stands for a 1–0 American victory.

The following day at Nagoya the Americans had to rally for three runs in the eighth inning to edge their rivals, 6–5. As the competition drew closer, there were some nationalistic chants, but they were drowned out by repeated applause for the American players.

Connie Mack believed that great Japanese teams were imminent. He cited the several close games and foresaw the time when a "true world series" would be played, encompassing teams from America and Japan. It would be played on both continents, he prophesied.

In a speech before the America-Japan Society, Prince Iyesato Tokugawa told the visiting athletes:

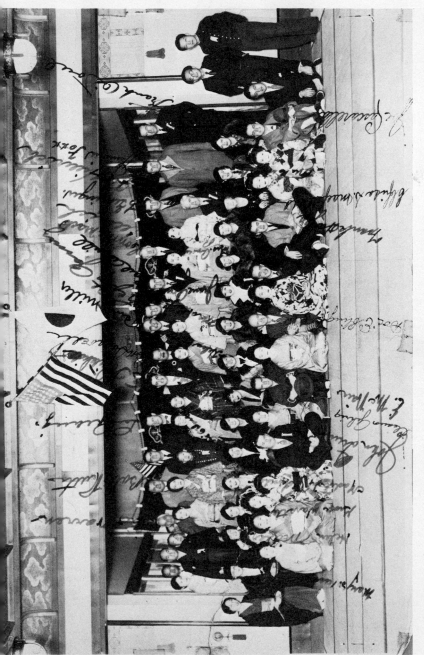

American all-star baseball players, wives, and their Japanese hosts, during the 1934 tour of Japan. Moe Berg is at the rear between Babe Ruth and Lou Gehrig.

American and Japanese all-star baseball teams posed for this picture prior to the first game of the 1934 series in

Babe Ruth, Moe Berg, and Lefty O'Doul with unidentified Japanese hosts in 1934.

Moe Berg and his friend, Takizo "Frank" Matsumoto, in 1934. At right is New York Yankee slugger Lou Gehrig.

Moe and Takizo Matsumoto, left, with unidentified friend.

Moe, rear center, with friends in Japan. Baseball great Jimmy Foxx is at Berg's right.

"No longer is it possible for you Americans to claim baseball as the national game of America alone. Today we feel we have the right to claim it also as the national game of Japan.

"Between the two great peoples who can really understand and enjoy baseball, there can be no national differences or diplomatic complications which cannot be solved in the same spirit of sportsmanship and fair play."

Two years later, under Shoriki's leadership, Japan would field seven professional baseball teams. Attendance at games in Japan's major cities was comparable to those in America's major league baseball cities.

During the last week of the tour, Berg played little, and Frank Hayes of Philadelphia did most of the catching. Berg was almost always in the bullpen.

Moe did miss several social functions as the tour continued into late November.

On November 27, he read headlines in the Japanese press that France was prepared to yield the Saar Basin to Hitler. With even greater interest, however, he read that Ambassador Grew's daughter, Mrs. Cecil Burton Lyon, who was married to the third secretary in the American Embassy at Peking, had given birth to a girl at St. Luke's International Hospital in Tokyo. The hospital towered above most of the city.

Two days later, on Friday, November 29, the Omiya Grounds, seventeen miles north of Tokyo, was jammed for the American-Japanese all-star game. Moe Berg was missing from the ball park. Shortly after the game began, Moe Berg walked through crowded Tokyo streets wearing a black kimono. It was a clear day and he walked briskly.

At Omiya, Charlie Gehringer rammed a long home run to left field to put the Americans in the lead. Fast-ball pitcher Takeda was on the mound for Japan.

In Tokyo, Berg continued walking, entered a florist shop, and bought a bouquet of fall flowers. He carried the flowers several blocks, carefully keeping the wrapping over them. He then waved for a cab and asked to be taken to St. Luke's International Hospital.

In Omiya Babe Ruth drew a huge "banzai" and rewarded his idols with a home run to deep center field.

In Tokyo, Moe Berg entered St. Luke's and went immediately to the reception desk; the flowers were now exposed. Speaking in Japanese, he told a nurse he was a friend of Ambassador Grew's daughter, Mrs. Lyon, and wanted to visit her. The nurse directed him to an elevator and said Mrs. Lyon was on the seventh floor. As he entered the elevator, Berg spotted security officials in the lobby.

He left the elevator on the seventh floor, observed several doctors and nurses and other hospital personnel moving about. He talked to no one as he walked down a corridor, flowers in hand, toward an exit to the stairwell. Confident that no one was watching him, Berg moved through the door. He scaled the stairs to a rooftop door and promptly pushed it open. He closed the door behind him and placed the flowers on the hospital roof. From

inside his kimono he took a motion picture camera that
had been strapped to his body.

In Omiya cheers erupted as hard-hitting Japanese center
fielder Horio homered in the sixth inning to give Japan a
temporary 5–4 lead.

In Tokyo, Moe Berg raised the camera to his eye and
began filming. He scanned the maze of structures that
housed and employed five and a half million Japanese. He
filmed low-level industrial complexes and armament
plants, oil refineries and railroad lines, the Imperial Palace
and warships in Tokyo Bay.

The city was Berg's priority but he also pointed the
camera toward the distant contours on the periphery. He
swept the black camera toward Musashino, Mitaka and
Togochi and Hoya in the west, where snow-capped Fuji
gleamed seventy-three miles in the distance. He aimed the
camera to the south, where the outline of Yokohama could
be seen. He captured Funabashi and Narashino on the
eastern shores of Tokyo Bay. He turned and aimed northward toward Kawaguchi, Matsudo and Suko.

In Omiya, Charlie Gehringer cracked his second home
run of the game to ignite a United States rally and an
eventual 23–5 victory.

Atop St. Luke's Hospital Moe Berg attached the camera
to his body, picked up the flowers, and carefully placed
them inside his kimono.

Berg never saw and never met Mrs. Lyon.

Approximately seven and one-half years later, military intelligence removed Moe Berg's films from their resting place. They were designated to be among the chief photographs used in the massive air raids against Tokyo in World War II. They were initially employed in the preparation of General Jimmy Doolittle's attack on the Japanese mainland from the carrier U.S.S. *Hornet*.

The April 18, 1942, raid was the first against the Japanese mainland during World War II and heartened an America still wounded by the defeat at Pearl Harbor.

2
The Family

MOE BERG WAS BORN March 2, 1902, in a cold-water tenement on East 121st Street, New York City, the second son
of Bernard and Rose Tashker Berg, immigrants from the
Ukraine. His father was among the waves of Russian immigrants who fled the pogroms that swept his native land
in the wake of Czar Alexander II's assassination. He escaped in 1894, leaving behind his family and fiancée, Rose,
whom he promised to bring to America when he had
raised enough money.

Bernard's father, Mendel Berg, reared his family of
three boys and three girls in the small Ukrainian town of
Kamanets, forty miles from the Rumanian border. A reserved, literary man, he worked as a bookkeeper in a grain
mill. The youngest son, Bernard had displayed the keenest
intellect and was allowed to enter public school, a rare
accomplishment for a Russian Jew in that era. He combined his public education and its loyalties to Russian history and philosophy with the vigorous, private study of
English.

In the midst of Bernard's schooling, his father lost several fingers while repairing a machine. He was forced to leave his job, so the family opened a small tavern and store. The money derived from this enterprise, coupled with Bernard's new job instructing village children, held the family together.

When Bernard first saw his future wife, Rose, he asked a mutual friend to arrange an introduction. An attractive dark-haired girl from the nearby village of Zaleshchiki, Rose was the second daughter in a family of seven children. Her father, Simon Tashker, was an educated man and an accountant in a large distillery owned by Russian nobility. Within a year of their meeting, Rose, twenty, and Bernard, twenty-four, were engaged. They decided their future lay in America.

With the aid of twenty dollars given him by his father-in-law, Bernard left the despair of the agrarian Ukraine for America. Smuggled over the border into Rumania, he made his way westward. His passage across the Atlantic aboard a Dutch ship, herded together in steerage with other immigrants, cost ten dollars. The aroma of cheese and bologna permeated the lower decks as hundreds slept on blankets for the sixteen-day crossing to the land of dreams. He arrived in America with ten dollars.

"When my father saw the tenements in the Lower East Side he got sick," Samuel Berg relates. "So intense was his outrage at the plight of American immigrants that he decided to try his luck in England. Fundless, he worked his way back across the ocean as a cowhand on a cattle freighter bound for London.

"My father lived with a cousin in Petticoat Lane in the

Moe's father, Bernard, as he looked shortly after his arrival in America.

Rose Tashker Berg, Moe's mother, soon after she came to the United States.

city's ghetto, near Soho. Just as my father arrived, a money panic and mild depression began. Unable to find work, he tried to enlist in the British army, rationalizing that at least it was a job, but he was rejected because he was an alien. Rather than return to Russia or live in another foreign country, he returned to the United States, this time working as a coal stoker on a freighter."

Once again in New York, Bernard swallowed his pride and moved into a tenement on Rivington Street, on the Lower East Side. He found a job making jewelry boxes and then ironed shirts in a laundry. Sustained by a strong will and unshakable determination, he managed to save a small sum of money. He sent ten dollars to Rose and asked her to join him. Her father buttressed this amount with a small dowry and a warning to be careful in her flight from Russia.

Rose left Zaleshchiki accompanied by a young girl, the daughter of a neighboring family, whom she was to escort safely to America. Taking only the barest of necessities, the pair moved southwesterly toward Rumania, carefully avoiding police patrols. On the eastern slopes of the Carpathian Mountains, they hugged the banks of the Siret River, which ultimately would lead them into Rumania.

At a prearranged point the pair met a professional river-crosser, who helped emigrants across the Siret at critical points for safe travel southward.

"My mother and the young girl had to be carried on the back of some man as they crossed the river to smuggle into Rumania," Dr. Berg continues. "My mother never forgot that."

Once in Rumania the pair took a train to Holland,

where they boarded the S.S. *Rotterdam* for the steerage trip to America. Bernard met Rose as she disembarked in New York.

A few months later, in January 1897, they were married. Rose worked as a seamstress until they earned sufficient money to open their own laundry on Ludlow Street, on the Lower East Side. Living quarters in the back were separated from the laundry by a curtain. Samuel Berg was born at that address.

"My mother would do the washing and ironing, all by hand, and my father would iron and deliver," Dr. Berg says. "He wanted to be a doctor but finances ruled that hope out. So he decided on pharmacy as an alternative."

While attending the Columbia College of Pharmacy, "My father studied from a bookstand when ironing shirts, but he scorched so many that my mother had to take over. After passing the New York State Board of Pharmacy examination, they moved to 121st Street, where my brother Moe was born. Then we moved to Newark, where my father felt a better environment existed."

In 1906, Bernard opened his first drugstore at Warren and Second streets and in 1910 he bought a newly constructed house, with two stores below, at 92 South Thirteenth Street in Newark, where he worked for the next thirty-two years.

"My parents were terribly anxious for me to enter school. When we moved to Newark they asked other parents in the neighborhood where their children attended school. The neighborhood was mostly Irish and the children attended St. Joseph's, so that's where I went. When my mother came to pick me up after school, she noticed

Moe at four.

Samuel Berg at four.

the nuns and told my father. After a week I went to public school."

At age three Moe Berg began to display athletic tendencies. Anything that was throwable sailed through the Berg household or in front of the pharmacy. One year later his batterymate on Thirteenth Street was the beat policeman, Officer Walter Hibler. Moe would move into catching position behind a manhole cover that served as home plate and Officer Hibler, wearing the colors of the Newark Police Department — derby hat, long, blue coat with accompanying badge, and a mild paunch — would begin to throw.

"There wasn't much traffic in the streets in those days, mostly pushcarts and horses," Dr. Berg remembers. "Moe would holler to Hibler 'Throw harder, harder.' The derby would fall off Hibler's head and no matter how hard he'd throw the ball, Moe would catch it without ever being knocked over. Crowds gathered to watch them."

Moe's ballplaying proficiency, at age seven, caught the attention of Newark's Rose Methodist Church baseball team. Its coaches enlisted Moe's services but religion, lacking ecumenical spirit in that era, dictated that Moe change his name. He played for Rose Methodist as Runt Wolfe.

In 1909 Moe's "ringer" pseudonym was mentioned publicly for the first time in the *Newark Evening News* sports section. The headline over a two-paragraph story read, WOLFE STAR IN CHURCH GAME. The story read, "Runt Wolfe starred in the contest between the Rose M. E. Church A team and the High Street Presbyterian nine yesterday at Weequahic Park, the former winning 9 to 7.

"Runt laid down a bunt in the ninth inning, sending in

the tying run, and a few minutes later scored himself with what proved to be the winning tally."

Playing baseball was an unbreakable habit for Moe in his youth. The drugstore operated from 8 A.M. to 11 P.M. but he contributed little in terms of assistance to his father, who was dismayed by his son's devotion to the sport.

"Moe was simply a genetic deviant," says Samuel Berg. "The Berg family tree shows it produced about twenty-five doctors in North and South America during the first half of this century, but Moe didn't like the sight of blood. Ever since he was two years old it was 'Hey Sam, let's catch.' It could be a ball, an orange, anything."

After spending the day at South Eighth Street public school, where the only criticism of his schoolwork was his off-key singing, dutifully noted in his report card, Moe ran off to play ball. Seldom would he return home before dark. His baseball addiction once prompted a family dispute. Moe retaliated by running away from home, and hours later was found wandering with a baseball bat slung over his shoulder.

The drugstore did well in its Roseville setting and much of the neighborhood traded there. The store generated a friendly atmosphere and its proprietor served as both pharmacist and sometime doctor. His strong personality, laced with understated humor, drew people to him. Samuel Berg recalls that many people came to the store seeking a laxative. The formula, often taken by distressed customers on the spot, became known as "Berg cocktails." Berg recalls a woman entering the pharmacy for such a cocktail.

"How far do you live from here, Mrs. Smith?" asked the pharmacist.

"Four blocks, Mr. Berg."

"Well, I'm going to give you a four-block Berg cocktail, which is very punctual. I want you to drink it all down here and leave immediately. And please, Mrs. Smith, don't stop to talk to anyone on the way home."

Newark, a melting pot of foreigners, enhanced the elder Berg's love of language. He developed into a capable linguist by borrowing the foreign-language books of his customers and speaking to them in their native tongue. He devoured books in a fashion Moe would soon emulate and surpass.

But Moe's father did not attempt to inculcate a love of languages in his sons. It was a natural, personal development for Moe that blossomed at Newark's Barringer High School, where his athletic prowess first began to attract extensive public notice. Moe played third base for the high school baseball club and was the team star. A *Newark Ledger* account of a game played April 18, 1918, between Barringer and East Orange reads: "For an early season game the contest was a hummer. The fierce rivalry between the teams had the players on their mettle and many were the dazzling stops and bullet throws during the contest. East Orange led 1 to o after the first inning. For the next seven innings neither team threatened at the plate. Barringer showed all her old indomitable spirit in the last inning. Berg, the Blue and White's mighty mauler, sent a screeching two-bagger to deep center. Captain Crooks followed this with a rousing hit for two bases, scoring Berg. King hit a hot one to Beckett, who guarded second for East Orange. Beckett juggled the ball and Crooks, taking a long chance, scored from second with what Barringer thought

Bernard Berg in front of his drugstore in Newark.

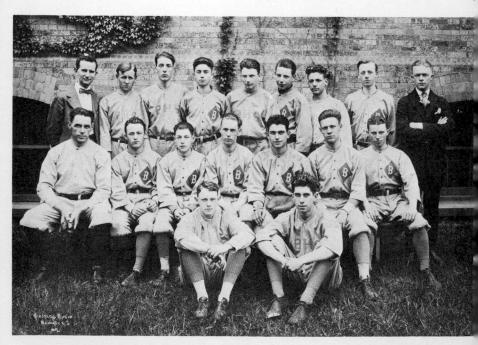

Barringer High School baseball team. Moe is in the last row, fourth from left.

was the winning run. East Orange retaliated with two runs in the bottom of the ninth inning to win 3 to 2."

When he wasn't on the base paths, Moe was a brilliant student at Barringer, and the study of languages now fascinated him and became his forte.

3
Princeton

Following his four years at Barringer, the budding scholar-athlete sought to further his education at New York University, where his brother Samuel was enrolled in premed school.

"Moe came to NYU because I was there," Dr. Berg recalls. But after two semesters, Moe decided to quit NYU and applied for admission to Princeton University.

Entrance to Princeton in that period was either extremely difficult or quite simple, depending upon the candidate's background. An applicant had to be either very smart or very rich. For Moe, who desired to major in modern languages, the entrance requirements were three years of Greek, four years of Latin and three years of English. In addition, he had to hurdle formidable College Board examinations. He was tested on his translation of Homer and Cicero into English, as well as English passages into Greek and Latin.

When Moe was informed he had been accepted at

Princeton, his family was elated. Moe's father was particularly pleased that his younger son was heading toward the teaching profession at one of the country's finest institutions of higher learning.

Moe's class was the first to enter Princeton after World War I. It was a period of optimism. The "best of all possible worlds" had arrived. There was never going to be another war and there would be two chickens in every pot. The Class of '23 was one of the largest ever to enroll at Old Nassau. There were about seven hundred freshmen, including ex-servicemen whose studies had been interrupted by the war. Approximately three hundred members of the class withdrew after freshman year, yielding to rigid Princeton academic standards.

Princeton unfolded a new world for Moe. The handsome campus clashed with the rough Roseville section of Newark. From Nassau Street to the banks of Lake Carnegie stood some of the most beautifully designed college buildings in America — majestic Gothic edifices resting among ancient elms. The sloping, grassy grounds — crisscrossed by cement walks — added to the bucolic serenity of the campus.

Nearly three-quarters of Moe's class came from prep schools. The majority of his classmates were sons of bankers, manufacturers, lawyers and physicians. A few of the celebrated rich were driven to school in limousines.

"We had more millionaires there than we had students," S. Lang Makrauer, a classmate of Moe's and now a Boston attorney, reminisces. "Moe was a high school boy as was I. Most of the other students were preppies. At that time at Princeton we had only two kinds of students: rich and poor. I was one of the poor ones. Moe, I think, had just enough to get by on."

Tuition was two hundred dollars a year in 1919. Room and board increased yearly costs to around six hundred and fifty dollars. In four years at Princeton, Moe supplemented what money his father could afford by working at a summer camp in New Hampshire and delivering mail during Christmas vacation. He was granted a nominal scholarship of one hundred and twenty-seven dollars for several years from the Orris Fund, set up for students of "good character and ability, of diligence, scholarship and exemplary behavior." Despite these sources of finance, Moe did not have sufficient funds to carry him through the four years. It was necessary for him to apply for a university loan, which he repaid the year following graduation.

Moe expressed his financial plight in a letter to his family on November 3, 1919:

Dear Folks,
    The light is fine. Just what I wanted. But, Pa, don't spoil your eyes on account of me. There's plenty of heat in my room. I'm wearing the smoking jacket now; just what I wanted. I wear the blue sweater (slip over) under my coat & feel perfectly comfortable. But now I have to break some hard news. I just got a bill from the Princeton Univ. Store to the amount of $31.90. It's pretty high but it includes everything I have bought, i.e., books (about 11), note books, regulation theme paper, etc. (to the am't of $15). Then I bought a class banner that covers one whole wall which everybody buys for $6.00. Add to this $8.00 for clothes pressing and $4.50 for Daily Princetonian. I paid for some in cash and brought it down to $31.90. But you can bet that I needed every bit of it and this is the last time I'll have a bill for a month of over a couple of dollars. It requires a little bit to get started. So, Pa, if you will

mail a check to me for $31.90, payable to the 'Princeton University Store,' everything'll be O.K. I hate like the dickens to write to you to do this but I have to. My expenses are curtailed now to a minimum. If I could leave to make the money I would. Good bye & don't work too hard.

Moe

Princeton's renowned language department had brought Moe to Old Nassau and his fascination and grasp of language showed immediately. "I was in at least one small class with Moe in our freshman year," recalls Crossan Cooper, a Baltimore attorney. "It was a Latin class. The only people in the class were the ones who received the highest marks on the College Board examinations in Latin. Moe was one of the outstanding stars in that class. He almost spoke Latin at that time."

Moe's linguistic prowess blossomed under the tutelage of Dr. Christian Gauss, chairman of the Department of Modern Languages, who was his faculty adviser, and Professor Harold H. Bender, philologist and etymologist, who was professor of Indo-Germanic philology and was later named chairman of Princeton's Department of Oriental Languages and Literature. "Moe had Bender for four years," Makrauer recalls. "Bender was his big scholastic influence and hero on campus. Bender was a great scholar and recognized in Moe a real talent for languages."

Often, the professor and his prodigy would huddle in the university library or in Bender's office, spending hours tracing words from their original Latin and Greek into other languages.

Moe took six courses per term, an unusually heavy load, and virtually all were language courses. He took two and a half years of Latin, four years of French, two and a half years of Spanish, three years of Italian, a year of Greek, a year of German, and a course in Sanskrit. He read the works of famous authors in their original languages. His sharp ears were attuned to the rich and subtle inflections of modern tongues, and by his senior year, Moe was speaking Italian, French, Spanish and German with remarkable authority.

"If you saw him when he spoke Italian, you would swear he was Italian," says Makrauer. "Same was true when he spoke French, or Spanish or German."

According to Samuel Berg, French was Moe's favorite language. "He loved the sounds of that language and speaking it."

Moe's insatiable curiosity for languages prompted vigorous study of ancient Sanskrit. "Moe developed his interest in Sanskrit from Bender, who was a great student of the language," Makrauer continues. "With Bender's guidance, Moe actually could read Sanskrit and write it."

Moe often studied in his dormitory room at Reunion Hall, where he lived alone his freshman year. In his sophomore year he lived with a high school friend, Raymond Sutton, Class of '22, at Williams Place. He and Sutton roomed together again the following year at 6 South West, where Moe lived alone his senior year.

Moe won general honors in his first, second and third years, but "I never saw him carrying a book while we were at Princeton," Makrauer states. Another classmate, Gelston Hardy, says, "I can't recall a single case where he was called on for an answer and he didn't have it."

Sutton adds, "Things came very easily to Moe. He had a retentive memory. He took copious notes. He never wasted any time. Moe was tremendously well liked by the baseball players. Some of them came to him for help with their studies. As his roommate, I witnessed him willingly giving his time to help them with their studies. He enjoyed doing it. At night, we always took a good walk before going to bed."

There was very little social life at Princeton then. There were no women among the two thousand students enrolled, and the town of Princeton, whose main street faces the campus, closed down well before midnight.

"There was no night life in Princeton except going to the movies," recalls Cooper. "There weren't many girls around town at the time. As far as I knew, Moe never dated anyone. Matter of fact, none of us did much."

Moe kept pretty much to himself and was regarded as a loner. "Moe was a man of mystery," Don Griffin, another classmate and resident of Princeton, remembers. "No one could quite account for all the things he did and the places he went. He traveled alone most of the time and you never saw him with anyone."

Hardy adds, "He was very mysterious. He was like a Cheshire cat — excellent at simply disappearing."

"Yes, he was a loner," Makrauer agrees, "but remember, here's a guy coming from a high school and seeing these other guys running around in their fancy clothes. This was an atmosphere new to Moe. He was a little snowed by it, but he was never antiestablishment. He was never resentful or envious of the rich students. Quite the contrary, he got along well with those boys and they respected him. But it was the athletes he felt more comfortable with. He stuck pretty close to the athletes."

Moe's exploits on the baseball field catapulted him to a position among the most celebrated college players of his era.

"He was a sensational baseball player," recalls Griffin. "There were two baseball players in this area we remember best. One was the Fordham Flash, Frankie Frisch, and the other was Moe Berg. Moe's name was just common conversation for everybody."

College baseball was very popular during Moe's Princeton years. It was virtually on a par with football. When Princeton played arch rivals Harvard and Yale, attendance sometimes reached as high as twenty thousand. "You could expect three hundred people out in the stands at University Field just to watch the team work out," Griffin says.

Moe played shortstop on the varsity. The other end of the double-play combination in his senior year was Cooper, who, like Moe, spoke Latin. The pair would practice Latin on the playing field, shouting phrases at one another.

"Sometimes we did it to confuse the opponents," Cooper said. "Moe and I would shout 'your turn' or 'my turn' in Latin so that the other side would not know which of us was going to cover second base on a given play. Of course, we assumed the first base coach for the other side didn't understand Latin."

In Moe's junior year, the Princeton baseball team was an exceptionally good one. It played the world champion New York Giants in an exhibition game in 1922 and almost beat them.

"We played them at the Polo Grounds," Cooper recounts. "I remember one play in which the batter hit a

The Princeton baseball team of 1921. Moe Berg is in the second row, second from right. Coach William Clarke is in the front row, third from left.

wicked line shot on one hop to Jack Jeffries, who was playing right field for us, and the ball was hit so hard and traveled so fast Jeffries was able to fire a throw to first and beat the runner for an out. John McGraw, the Giants manager, was sitting outside the dugout on a chair and when he saw that play he got up and said, 'Well, I'm a sonuvabitch!'

"Trudeau Thomas was pitching for us that day. He had a great curve ball and was going great guns. We were ahead 2–1 in the last of the ninth. They had a man on third with two out. The batter hit a pop fly in the area of the mound and Thomas moved under the ball to catch it and end the game. Cozy Dolan was coaching at first for the Giants and as the ball came down he yelled, 'I got it! I got it!' Thomas backed away, thinking one of his infielders would catch the ball, and it dropped in for a hit, scoring the runner from third. The Giants got another run to beat us."

After the game, McGraw invited some of the Princeton team, including Berg and Cooper, and its coach, Bill Clarke, to dinner. Later, McGraw walked the Princeton contingent to Grand Central Station, where they were to board a train for the university. Giving his farewell, McGraw said, "Well, good night boys. You were almost champs of the world today."

That team, according to Cooper, "was not half as good as the one the year later." Records attest to that. In Moe's senior year, the Princeton baseball team authored a record nineteen straight victories.

Moe's batting average of .386 that year was the highest on the team, and his only shortcoming was lack of speed. Coach Clarke invariably placed him at or near the bottom of the batting order to balance the team's offense.

The combination of Moe's linguistic and athletic accomplishments made him one of the best-known students on campus, but, though he admired much of what the university represented, he also learned of its cruel side — discrimination — and this would have a lasting impact on his life.

The incident that most affected Moe occurred in his sophomore year and involved the socially prestigious eating clubs for upperclassmen. There were three clubs the athletes favored: Tiger Inn, Elms, and Cannon. In order for sophomores to join, members had to approve. Students from minority groups or others who didn't "fit" were often overlooked.

"Right after we had taken our midterms for the sophomore year, the club elections took place," Makrauer recalls. "The clubs at the time Moe and I were there were a very, very important thing on campus. They weren't fraternities. They were eating clubs and they were very special.

"Moe had a great friend in Jack Jeffries, who was captain of the baseball team and a fine athlete. Jeffries, of course, was bid a club by practically all those on campus and finally ended up by deciding to go Cannon. But Jeffries was not going unless Moe went.

"This started quite a to-do because, really, back then Princeton was not a tolerant place. Those guys were intolerant as hell. If you were blackballed by any one member of the club, you could not get in. The upperclassmen were willing to take Moe because they wanted Jeffries, so, they said they would take Moe providing he did not try to get any other Jews in.

"Moe told them what they could do with their clubs. Jack did not want to join without Moe, but not to make a federal case of it, Moe prevailed upon Jack to join. They would have taken Moe on their terms, but he was not buying that deal. Moe confirmed to me he was hurt by this club stuff."

Moe never returned for a class reunion. His only trips back to the campus were to visit individual friends or for a lecture or athletic contests.

Other classmates hold differing opinions as to why Moe did not join a club. Griffin believes, "Moe avoided the clubs. To my best knowledge, he may have been sensitive about the issue. He may have been thinking he might have been turned down. He hid from it, so it never really came up.

"I know there are people in our class who think he was

not elected to an eating club because he was a Jew and they point a finger at Princeton in those days as being anti-Semitic and other things, which is a subject in itself. If he had exposed himself to the Princeton tradition, he would have been in a club. In those days you always spoke to everybody else. The campus was friendly. Moe didn't fit this pattern. He was a loner."

Crossan Cooper remarks, "I don't think it was because he wasn't asked. I think Moe had enough friends in a number of clubs that he could have joined if he wanted to. The reason might have been financial because it was a little more expensive to eat in a club than in Commons."

Moe felt disdain for any form of ethnic differentiation. When the noted rabbi Stephen Wise visited Princeton in an effort to start a Jewish group on campus, Moe declined to join.

"Rabbi Wise came after us like Moses storming down from Mount Sinai," Makrauer recalls. "He had a voice on him like a violin and he knew how to play it. He spoke beautifully. He called for me and Berg. I ran over to Murray Dodge Hall to meet him. I had never seen the man, but I knew of him. My family consisted of Reformed Jews.

"Rabbi Wise said to me, 'Makrauer, I would like to start a Jewish group here to hold services Friday night.' My feeling was, we weren't there as Jews; we were there as students, and, if a guy wanted to go to the temple or to the synagogue, he could go.

"I said, 'No, thank you, Rabbi Wise.' I went to see Berg afterward and he said he had talked to Wise and also told him he was not interested.

"The thing was never organized. I suppose Wise thought

we were a couple of backsliders, but neither one of us pretended to be anything other than what we were. Make no mistake about that. In those days you had to put down what you were. Catholic. Jew. Presbyterian. Baptist. This information was put right in the book."

Moe graduated magna cum laude.

"I always said he was the brightest fellow in our class," Makrauer says, "and he always said I was. He didn't realize his full intellectual abilities until after he left Princeton."

4
Baseball

MOE BERG BEGAN his professional baseball career with the Brooklyn Dodgers of the National League in June 1923. He signed a five-thousand-dollar contract immediately after playing his last game for Princeton against Yale in Yankee Stadium. Yale won 5–1.

Considerable indecision preceded the signing. Despite his fondness for baseball and his obvious ability, Moe lacked the confidence that he could survive in the major leagues. Baseball and longevity did not go hand in hand and Berg knew that athletic talent died at an early age.

Berg's first priority, he told Princeton friends, was to further his education. He wanted to attend the Sorbonne in Paris to study experimental phonetics and philology under the renowned scholar Abbé Jean Pierre Rousselot but lacked the necessary money. Added frustration developed when Princeton offered him a teaching post in its Romance languages department.

Moe sought advice from two sources. Foremost, wrote

Arthur Daley of the *New York Times*, "the man who diverted Moe into baseball was Dutch Carter, the eminent lawyer. Carter once had pitched so superbly for Yale that big league teams clamored for his services.

'Take the baseball career,' said Dutch. 'The rest can wait. When I was your age I had a chance to pitch in the National League. But my family looked down on professional sports and vehemently opposed my accepting. I've always been sorry I listened to them, because it made me a frustrated man. Don't you become frustrated. At least give it a try.' "

Moe then went to Coach Clarke, who theorized that playing in the major leagues was the equivalent of being President. He felt Moe had the potential for baseball greatness and reasoned that the five thousand dollars would pay for Sorbonne study at the season's end. Berg was to tell sportswriters over the years that he waited in vain for a call from the White House seeking an exchange of jobs. "I guess all the Presidents were outfielders."

Twenty-four hours after his conference with Clarke, Moe stood on first base in Shibe Park in Philadelphia, home of the Phillies. In his first appearance at bat for the Dodgers, he singled to left field, driving in a run.

Coach Clarke and a small army of friends, sitting among 1520 fans, stood up and cheered. So did some of the seasoned baseball types in the Brooklyn dugout, including legendary Dazzy Vance, Dutch Reuther, Zack Wheat and Charley "Boss" Schmidt.

In reporting Berg's first professional game, the *New York Herald* said:

"So easy were the Phillies today that when the Brooklyn

Dodgers took the first game of the series by 15 to 5 Manager Wilbert Robinson gave his second string men a chance to work out.

"The most conspicuous of the second string men was Moe Berg, who until last night was an amateur in good standing on the Princeton nine.

"When the Dodgers had built up a lead of 13 to 4 in their first seven innings Manager Robinson thought the opportunity ripe to see what Berg could do. Berg had been recommended by Robinson's old sidekick, Bill Clarke, Princeton coach and former assistant catcher to Robbie on the Baltimore Orioles of hallowed memory.

"Moe fielded in the seventh without incident. He batted in Olson's place in the eighth and scratched a single over Clarence Mitchell's head, scoring Taylor. He came up in the ninth inning and flied to Lee in right field. He is a right-handed batter. In the field Moe had three put outs and two assists. He caught a hard liner from Cy Williams in the Philadelphia ninth with Mokan on first and threw to Fournier doubling up Mokan and ending the game."

Manager Robinson tested Berg further. He dictated that Moe was to room with Schmidt, whose baseball reputation suggested gladiatorial capabilities. An attraction of opposites immediately developed. Berg reveled in the company of Schmidt's boisterousness, while the veteran athlete found a sense of excitement and a strain of delicacy in the new Brooklyn shortstop that calmed his temper.

Berg would recall that Schmidt thought it madness to go to Paris "to study about goddam words of a thousand years ago. Hell, Moe, don't you know what Paris is for?"

Berg inundated their room with dozens of foreign-language newspapers, as Schmidt looked on incredulously. Any attempt by Schmidt to scrutinize one would incite a Berg censure.

"Charlie, don't touch them. Those papers are alive. I haven't read them. When I'm through reading them they'll be dead and you can have them."

Throughout Berg's lifetime it was forbidden to touch his newspapers before he read them. When a violation occurred he would discard the tainted paper and walk through a snowstorm, if need be, to purchase a new one. Newspapers provided the fastest form of information for Berg. His fetish for them, which began in an era that lacked vast networks of communication, never subsided. Indeed, it increased with passing years.

Moe once explained, "I read newspapers because they instruct me as to what is going on. There is, really, no alternative to them, and I seek none. There is a majesty about the printed word. There is life to it. I consider a newspaper a friend. My only demand is that it report to me well. Great writing is not essential, but the truth is."

Berg played well for Brooklyn during his first season, but it was not a spectacular year. Critics marveled at his dazzling plays at shortstop, but cautioned that his lackluster hitting could doom him to the minor leagues. In forty-nine games, Moe hit .186, a mark unacceptable in major league competition.

Casey Stengel recalls:

"I was winning 'em for the Giants in those days when the young Berg fellah joined that Flatbush crowd.

"Now, I'll tell ya, Moe was a graceful shortstop; great arm, threw the ball like a bullet. He looked real marvel-

ous. But I'll tell ya somethin' else. He couldn't run. Bad
legs. A turtle could beat him to first base. If Moe got a two-
base hit, why the kid was in a marathon to get to second.
That's how it was.

"Moe was a very enlightened fellah, but nobody ever
knew his life's history. Never knew what he was up to. A
big question mark guy, but he kept the English language
alive for the ballplayers.

"He was always different from the other guys. I'd see
Moe take a drink once in a while. And I'll tell ya, he'd
walk into the place erect and walk out erect. That's an
example."

Berg provided sportswriters with an opportunity to
write different copy. In every major league city, writers
combined stories of Berg's playing ability with his linguistic accomplishments and Princetonian refinement.
These qualities were often weighed indelicately against
Berg's unlettered comrades. Such stories would come in
profusion during the next seventeen years and cause Berg
uneasiness.

"I have met many men in the major leagues who excel
over me in ways that I envy," Berg would offer. "Because I
speak a few languages does not place my abilities over
theirs. The joy of baseball is that a man must stand on his
two feet and face his opponents. Philology cannot assist me
in fielding a grounder flawlessly or help when I'm at the
plate, the bases are loaded, and my team is behind."

At season's end, Berg went to the Sorbonne to study
under Rousselot. There the classics took on a vibrant new
meaning. The Romance languages, with their centuries-

old impact on human thought and the spoken word, became a source of heightened excitement for Moe. He and Rousselot, virtually inseparable for six months, traced the bastardization of pure Latin as it mixed with the tongues of fallen nations. The philological paths taken by teacher and pupil spanned continents, and the evolution of words remained a consuming passion for Berg, who corresponded with Rousselot until the scholar's death.

Years later *Boston Herald* sports columnist Bill Cunningham asked Berg to discuss his Sorbonne year.

"Well, you see," Berg said, "we philologists are interested in a great many things. My original interest was in discovering where the irregular spellings and endings crept into the various languages. For instance, the farther Caesar's legions trekked from Rome, the more the pure Latin became diluted with the words and idioms of the people they were trying to subjugate. In one sense it's a breakdown, but true philologists consider it an evolution.

"For example, the Latin word for twenty is, as you know, 'viginti.' The modern word in French for the same thing is 'vingt.' To a philologist it's instantly apparent that the 'g' in vingt is in the wrong place. Tracing backwards we discover that before the Renaissance, 'viginti' had been corrupted or had developed into 'vint,' so far as the French were concerned.

"Scholars of the Renaissance, comparing the two, decided the word was being misspelled, and undertook to place the 'g' back in it. They simply got it in the wrong place, that's all. . . . And now you take the Latin word for horse. It's 'caballus.' It's represented in various languages by various words — cavalier, caballero, cavalry and so forth. In French, it became 'cheval.' Now the normal plural in almost any language is obtained by adding s or es. Furthermore the letters 'i' and 'u' are so interconnected in vocalic expression that they are almost interchangeable. Hence, in the spoken word, the plural of cheval becomes automatically something such as 'chevaus.'

"It was so spoken in French before printing presses were invented. Manuscript writers used symbols of a sort here and there. They fell into the habit of using a peculiar-looking one at the end of the word 'chevaus.' It had an upward flourish to it that made it look not unlike the letter 'x.' So when printing came along, the printers, looking for something to duplicate that symbol, simply selected the letter x, and that's how and why the plural of the French word cheval is chevaux. . . ."

Berg returned from France for 1924 spring training with the Dodgers and found himself, as anticipated, optioned to Minneapolis for the first half of that season. Then he was traded to Toledo for the remainder of the year. He played reasonably well for the two American Association clubs, getting a hundred and ten hits and batting .264.

When the 1925 baseball year began Berg was sent to the Reading Keys of the International League. Moe confided to friends that he intended to spend only the current year in the minor leagues. He wanted to reenter the major leagues or retire from baseball. The possibility of a professorship at Princeton loomed again.

Moe's baseball fortune rose at Reading. He developed into a brilliant hitter and his fielding at shortstop was compared to that of the premier players in the major leagues. He collected two hundred hits during the year, drove in a hundred and twenty-four runs, hit nine home runs, and batted a career high of .311.

Reading warned major league teams they would have to pay dearly for Berg. The Chicago White Sox and the New York Yankees were the two contenders. The White Sox, who had first option, bought him for approximately fifty thousand dollars, a significant sum at that time.

Berg failed to appear at spring training in 1926 and the White Sox learned that he had quietly entered Columbia Law School at the end of the previous season. He refused to join the club for six weeks, until school was over.

White Sox president Charles A. Comiskey wrote a "my dear young man" letter to Berg to determine whether baseball or law school was his priority. He contended that if education received Berg's nod, then he should forget baseball.

"The game was in my blood now and I hated to quit," Berg told interviewers.

A fortuitous incident at Columbia allowed Berg to pursue both careers. He went to Professor Noel Dowling to probe a point in law. Dowling was reading the sports pages when Berg entered his office. The professor commented gratuitously that the Giants had beaten Pittsburgh the day before, then proceeded to discuss baseball, unaware that Berg was a professional ballplayer. Dowling said he had played first base for Vanderbilt University.

"I played for Princeton," Moe said.

"Are you the Berg from Princeton?" asked Dowling. Berg responded yes, then both men discussed Moe's schedule dilemma. Professor Dowling produced a program allowing Moe to double up on courses immediately, clearing his path for spring training the following season.

Even while at Columbia Law School, Moe was upset when journalists compared his intellectual gifts to those of his teammates, and finally he lost his temper when a group of sportswriters went there to interview him.

Arthur J. Lea Mond, in his *Sports Intelligentsia* column, wrote: "How does it feel to be called the most intelligent man in sports?

"We wondered after hearing that Morris (Moe) Berg, of the White Sox had been adjudged that by a raft of newspapermen. So we decided to get in touch with Mr. Berg himself. We took the subway to Columbia University where he is studying law and found the gentleman in John Jay Hall. There he was sitting in an easy chair, coat and vest off and comfy slippers on his feet. He was reading some French novel — in the original.

"We talked of this and that, recalling some incidents of his early baseball career. Then, knowing the tall, well-proportioned athlete pretty well we popped the question:

" 'Well, Moe, how does it feel to be the most intelligent man in sports?'

"He grimaced and was on the verge of tossing a radiator at us. But he thought better of it.

" 'How do you get that way?' was his answer. And before we had a chance to interrogate further he added, 'You lay off that intelligence stuff. I've already heard too much of it. One gets fed up with some things you know.'

"So the conversation was switched and we kept it in one of the sixteen languages Moe speaks — English, also being our best. In the course of it, he was inclined to talk of baseball because he likes to play it and six-day bicycling races because he gets a two-fold kick out of it, watching the riders pedal around and from his talks with trainers of foreign cyclists.

"Berg is interesting but he never appears high brow and he fears, that by the various newspaper stories the world in general will get an idea that he is Tunneyesque."

Moe Berg knew he was fighting a losing battle with sportswriters. He privately theorized that stories alluding to his intellectuality would bore readers, who would judge him solely by his playing ability. The future would prove his theory wrong.

Three years after entering law school, Moe received his law degree, and after passing the New York State bar examination became an off-season lawyer with the Wall Street firm of Satterlee and Canfield, where his expertise in languages was often used in the handling of foreign contracts and international matters.

Berg saw limited shortstop service during his first season with the White Sox. He rode the White Sox bench, waiting for an opportunity to play and consuming the language idioms and provincialisms of ballplayers from scattered parts of the nation. On the ball field Moe intentionally, and with private joy, spiced his language with unorthodox contractions and double negatives.

He considered his reading and studies a private matter. He would rarely discuss them with other players, and, careful not to expose his scholarship beyond reason, Moe was found by most companions a trusted friend with a wit and style foreign to baseball. Sportscasters, however, would allude to Berg as the "professor," a reference he found embarrassing. But the word professor and the name Berg became synonymous throughout Moe's career.

"The score is tied, two men on base for the White Sox. Professor Berg at the plate. The professor struck out in the first inning, doubled in the third."

Berg became a catcher by accident when a series of mishaps depleted the White Sox catching staff over a four-day period in August of 1927. Manager-catcher Ray Schalk and his backup Frank Crouse had their fingers ripped in successive days in Philadelphia playing against the Athletics.

In Boston, third-string catcher Harry McCurdy had his thumb lashed by a Red Sox batter in the fifth inning. The White Sox bench was in an uproar. "My God, where the hell's the end to this nightmare?" Berg remembered Schalk screaming when he recounted the incident.

There was talk of calling the game off, an unusual consideration in major league baseball, but Berg went to Schalk and volunteered to catch. He said he had caught one game years ago in high school and pleaded that he could handle the situation.

"If the worse happens, kindly deliver the body to Newark," Berg said.

"One game in high school and you want to get behind the plate, Moe? You must be mad, but so am I. Good luck, kid."

As Berg outfitted in catcher's garb, several White Sox players walked over to shake his hand and muttered they hoped he'd survive. He tested several catchers' mitts at home plate as ballplayers, umpires and thousands in the stands gaped in suspended contemplation.

Berg caught surprisingly well for the rest of the game with only one base stolen off him when a ball he'd thrown got wedged beneath the second base bag and the ground. It was his first throw to second as a catcher. When he returned to the bench the players teased him that the ball is to be thrown above the base. He countered, "Now you tell me." The Red Sox won 4–1.

Hours later Moe Berg was on Boston Common among thousands gathered to protest a denial of a stay in the execution of Sacco and Vanzetti.

The White Sox next moved to Yankee Stadium for a series with the world champion Yankees. Ted Lyons was scheduled to pitch. There was indecision whether to place Berg behind the plate or use one of the injured catchers.

Lyons recalls, "I asked Schalk for Moe. I said he looked good in Boston and I was confident that he could do the job." Schalk agreed with his pitching ace.

Years later Moe related that when Babe Ruth came to bat for the first time in the game he looked down and said, "Moe, you're going to be the fourth wounded White Sox catcher by the fifth inning."

"I looked up at that marvelous round man," Berg continued, "and said that I would only call for inside pitches and we'd keep each other company at the hospital. We both laughed and then Lyons struck the Babe out."

Ruth struck out twice during the game and only Tony Lazzeri managed to steal a base. Lyons hurled an eight-hitter in a 6–3 White Sox victory. Berg had a single in four times at bat. After the last out, Berg rushed to Lyons and threw his arms around him then moved on to Manager Schalk and said, "Ray, thank you for letting me catch today."

"Thank me, Moe? I want to give you a kiss."

"Moe caught the damnedest game," recounts Lyons. "He was a big man and made a fine target. He had good actions and a strong arm and great hands. His signal calling was flawless and in the years he was to catch me I never waved off a sign; few pitchers did. He became clinical in studying batters, knew their weaknesses and strengths. He took full advantage of this and pitchers simply felt confident with Moe doing the catching. He was a remarkable handyman. He lacked only speed. I remember one game in which we were leading 3–2 in the ninth inning. Ben Chapman hit a single to left field and a base runner was trying to score the tying run. Our left-fielder, Bib Falk, threw to the plate and Moe got the ball on a short hop and tagged the runner out. His shortstop experience showed behind the plate. No catcher could pick up short hops like Moe could."

"The charm of Moe Berg," Lyons continues, "was that he unconsciously wove his qualities into everyone who came his way. Sort of an eternal impact, there was no escaping. That Moe was able to suddenly declare himself a catcher and become a good one was characteristic of the man. If he applied himself, Moe Berg could be whatever he chose to be. A lot of people tried to tell him what to do with his life and brain and he retreated from this. Moe Berg had to be his own man. He tried to be a run-of-the-mill guy. He was different because he was different. He made up for all the bores of the world. And he did it softly, stepping on no one."

Berg felt confident behind the plate in the games ahead. Manager Schalk thought he detected in Moe a natural catcher. The position rejuvenated his being; there could be no return to the infield. And there wasn't.

"I'm elated over becoming a catcher," Berg told his baseball colleagues. "Being allowed to catch is the biggest break I've ever had. I feel that I can catch better than I can play shortstop. I'm not fast on my feet and my arm has saved me lots of times as an infielder. I've never been able to stay in the lineup long enough to develop as a hitter.

"Catching isn't as hard for me, after playing the infield so long, as you might think. I hope it lasts."

Stengel observes: "Now, I'll tell ya. I mean Moe Berg was as smart a ballplayer as ever come along. Knew the legs wouldn't cooperate in the infield and when the catching job opened up he grabs a mask and puts it on and there he was. Guy never caught in his life and then goes behind the plate like Mickey Cochran. Now that's somethin'. But, I'll tell ya again, nobody ever knew his life's history. I call him the mystery catcher. Strangest fellah who ever put on a uniform."

Berg struggled unsuccessfully to improve his hitting. Returning to the bench one day after striking out for the second time, fellow catcher Crouse, in drawling accent, said, "Moe, I don't care how many of those degrees you have, you ain't learned to hit the curve ball any better than the rest of us."

Moe pleaded with White Sox pitchers to remain after ball games so that he could have hitting practice. He endured considerable early morning wrath when he forced pitchers out of bed to accompany him to Comiskey Park for additional batting sessions. There would be a further flow of expletives as he stopped on the way for foreign newspapers. Still more profanity erupted when he warned pitchers, "Don't touch, don't touch, they're alive."

Berg shared catching duties with Crouse, McCurdy and Schalk, but by mid-season of 1928 he was regarded as the best receiver on the club.

Berg functioned unobtrusively as a catcher, relying on diplomacy as the most productive method in handling umpires. He was never thrown out of a ball game in his long major league career. Players of the Berg era recall Moe's relationship with umpire Bill McGowan. Once, after a McGowan call that Berg and his pitcher didn't agree with, Moe turned around and said in his soft, bass voice, "Bill, I want you to know that you can umpire better with one eye closed than most umpires can umpire with two eyes. And I'll challenge any man who argues to the contrary."

McGowan responded by closing one eye behind his mask. Berg then moved closer to McGowan and blinked one eye through his mask. At any point during the game when Berg thought McGowan may have missed a pitch he would turn slowly and close one eye. McGowan would respond by bending toward the catcher and blinking one eye, reminding him of his umpire supremacy. Berg and McGowan winked at each other for twelve years, enduring the varied comments of batters.

Lyons recalls, "I was kicking over a pitch once and Moe knew the pitch could have been called either way. Bill Dineen was the umpire and he was about to throw me out of the game. Moe turned around and said something. I called Moe to the mound and asked him what he said to

Dineen. Moe replied, 'I said, Bill, why throw Lyons out of the game. You're absolutely correct, the pitch was a ball, not a strike.' I was a bit angry but I remained in the game and we won.''

Umpire Bill Grieve, who spent many years in the American League, said he found Moe a "gentle man who fought for his team in every way he knew. If Moe thought I made a bad call he would say softly, 'I think you missed that one, Bill.' He was a big man who performed with gentleness. He knew no other way.''

Boston Red Sox utility infielder Louis "Bozey" Berger recalls Moe Berg's early catching psychology: "We were in Chicago for a series and I had never met Moe Berg before. He was catching for the White Sox and I stepped up to home plate to bat. Before the first pitch was thrown I heard a very low, almost mysterious voice coming from behind the catcher's mask. 'Bozey,' said Moe, 'is everything all right at home? How's your dear mother and how's your father?' ''

It was a brilliant year for Berg. He hit consistently, winning several games with critical hits, most of them hugging the left field line he favored.

He made only seven errors to lead catchers in defensive ability. His one hundred and one base hits in one hundred and seven games earned a .287 batting mark. Suddenly, Moe was among the best catchers in baseball. Of the twenty-five American League players who received votes for the Most Valuable Player award for 1929, Moe received two votes. Bill Dickey of the Yankees, the only other catcher to garner most valuable votes, received six. Al Simmons of Philadelphia won the top honor.

Berg's biggest faux pas as a catcher occurred in Washington while catching Alphonse "Tommy" Thomas. The White Sox and Senators were tied, 1–1, in the bottom of the eighth inning. The Senators had a runner on third base with one out.

Thomas remembers, "I got the next batter to hit a high foul near the home bench and Moe had to run a long way toward it and he made a darned good catch. I had run to cover home plate so that the runner on third wouldn't attempt to run home after the catch. Then something happened that I've never seen before and probably won't happen again. As soon as Moe caught the ball, he flipped it behind his back toward the pitching mound. He failed to realize that there were only two outs. And while the ball was resting on the unattended mound the Washington runner on third base ran home to give the Senators a 2–1 lead, and that's the way the game ended. The look on Moe's face as the winning run scored should have been recorded for posterity. Moe felt terrible, of course, and he never forgot that play."

Ballplayers throughout the league and sportswriters chided Berg for weeks, maintaining that in his intellectual pursuits he never learned how to count to three.

Moe's newfound baseball success prompted additional inquiry into his scholarship. Sitting before his locker, sweat still pouring, he would often be approached by mildly apologetic writers saying their editors insisted on a story regarding Moe's charter membership in the American Linguistic Society or one pertaining to his thesis on Sanskrit, which had been placed in the Library of Congress.

A protesting Berg would contribute the basics of Hindu

Opening Day game in 1929 for the White Sox at Comiskey Park, Chicago. Moe is fifth from left. Others in the photo are, from the left, Bob Weiland, pitcher; unidentified man in overcoat; Bill Cissell, shortstop; Art Shires, first baseman; Ted Blankenship, pitcher; Grady Adkins, pitcher; Martin "Chick" Autry, catcher; Alphonse "Tommy" Thomas, pitcher; Johnny Watwood, outfielder; Clyde "Buck" Crouse, catcher; Dan Dufan, pitcher; Willie Kamm, third baseman; Howard "Dupey" Redfern, infielder; and Ed Walsh, pitcher.

Moe provides a big target for the pitcher during warm-up practice prior to
the White Sox exhibition game at Indianapolis in 1929.

tongues and philosophy. He would baffle the uninitiated scribes with the knowledge that "the literature of ancient India is divided into the Sanskrit and the Veda as far back as two thousand years B.C. The Veda is the early form of Sanskirt and Vedic literature involves three prominent types, the Sutras, Brahmanas and the Samhitas. Its germane subdivisions are the Traya Vidya, or the threefold knowledge of the hymns of praise, the Rig Veda, involving chanted songs, and the Sama Veda." Moe would always break off such interviews with, "Thank you gentlemen, now I have to rest the body, rest the body." Sportswriters would leave, prepared for baffled looks from their city or sports desks.

Berg displayed a sense of humor and a strain of fatalism in discussing his language world. "I do it for the excitement that language generates. It is my hobby, nothing more. I firmly believe that no man is bilingual. Further, life is crowded with vagaries. I spend years attempting to master a number of foreign languages and what happens? I turn out to be a catcher and am reduced to sign language on the ballfield."

Berg practiced law at the end of the year. He found greater joy in studying old English law and its impact on world civilization than in the day-to-day ritual of contracts, briefs and courtroom procedures. But law enhanced his salary as the Great Depression cut fiercely into the nation's economic and moral strength.

Springtime and its summons for ballplayers to head south was welcomed by Moe in 1930. Efforts by other American League clubs to lure him from the White Sox were rejected. Good catchers were at a premium.

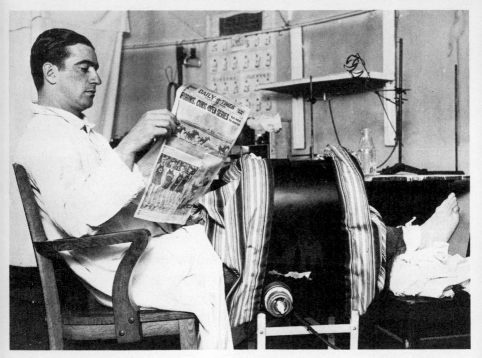

Moe underwent daily treatment for his knee, which he injured in spring training in 1930. Here he is shown with the knee in a baking machine at the University of Chicago. The mishap was costly. Berg never regained his hitting prowess of the 1929 season, when he batted .286.

One week before opening day in Chicago, Moe Berg singled against the New York Giants in an exhibition game at Little Rock, Arkansas. He moved off first base feigning a move to steal second. In an attempt to get back to first to beat a pick-off play, Moe's spikes caught and he crawled, in serious pain, back to the base. Ligaments below his right knee were ruptured badly.

The White Sox rushed Berg to Our Lady of Mercy Hospital in Chicago for surgery. The club held guarded optimism that he could return to the lineup in a month.

While at Mercy, Moe became a favorite with the nuns. Tommy Thomas recalls, "The nuns at Mercy thought there was no one like Moe Berg. They came in virtual shifts to enjoy this fellow who paraded the world through that hospital room. I'm not sure whether other patients received care while Moe Berg was there. When Moe left the hospital, two of the nuns who attended him at Mercy were later assigned to Des Moines and, apparently, were upset. They wrote a letter to Moe pleading with him to intervene, diplomatically, with the bishop. They wanted out of Des Moines and back to Chicago."

Berg left Mercy Hospital depressed. He sensed his leg would never be the same, and it wasn't. He had never been a fast runner on the bases and now he faced the realization that he would be even slower. He correctly suspected that he could never again reach the impressive playing standards he attained during the 1929 season. Berg's athletic career was derailed further when he developed bronchial pneumonia soon after his release from the hospital.

Moe played only twenty games for the White Sox during that grim season. In the spring of 1931, suspecting that Moe's best playing days were over, the White Sox sold Berg to the Cleveland Indians. The Indians already had three capable catchers in Luke Sewell, Glynn Myatt, and Joe Spring. Berg was destined to play little.

It was at this point in Berg's career that he became the sometimes catcher. He could remain in the bullpen for weeks without being called upon to catch a game. Berg did not resent the role. He found creativity in handling young pitchers and catchers. His baseball acumen was regarded as unexcelled and this would be his strength for the next ten years.

Bergian legends would develop from his bullpen residency. He became the bullpen general, its raconteur, its quiet man of contemplation, and, with each succeeding year, its gentle, withdrawn mystic.

Away from the ball field Berg studied languages with greater ferocity. He particularly concerned himself with the evolution of medieval French into modern French. Woven into his interests, enigmatically, was the world of the military. He consumed the military history of world civilizations.

Berg played in only ten games for Cleveland during the 1931 season, getting one hit in ten times at bat; this prompted a basically unfair assessment of Moe's hitting by writers who for years would suggest, "Moe Berg can speak twelve languages flawlessly and can hit in none." The Indians gave Moe his release at the end of the 1931 season. He was immediately signed by the Washington Senators, whose player-manager, Joe Cronin, was masterminding a huge effort to dethrone the New York Yankees as world champions. The signing of Berg began a long, close relationship between the catcher and Cronin in Washington and Boston.

"Baseball had few more memorable ballplayers than Moe Berg," Cronin says. "He was a living university in a baseball uniform. He loved the game and was a smart ballplayer. That's why I wanted him on my team. He had a great influence on a club, knew how to handle men. Moe was the only man I know of who could sit on the bench for two months, then be brought into a game and catch perfectly. I would wave him in from the bullpen. Moe would approach me in the dugout and ask if the rules of the game were still the same and if everyone still got three strikes due them. Then, with a big smile on his face, he would get behind the plate hollering encouragement to the players.

"The important aspect was that Moe could handle everyone. We had a pitcher on the Washington club named Earl Whitehill. He was a fiery left-hander. Wanted to win, wanted to win. And he was tough on the ball field. He wanted to beat you any way he could and it didn't make any difference who he was playing against. I generally wanted Moe to catch Whitehill and handle his fiery disposition. Moe had a huge influence on him and Whitehill had a deep respect for Moe. They complemented each other in a game. And, generally, they were a winning combination."

Moe Berg played more with Washington than he anticipated. His bullpen image was discarded briefly when Cronin ordered him behind the plate to catch seventy-five games in 1932. Moe hit .246 for the season, winning several games for the Senators with clutch hits. There were early season hopes of winning the pennant. In May, Cronin put Berg behind the plate to catch a series against the White Sox. In one of the games, Berg's former batterymate Ted Lyons was still on the mound in the fourteenth inning with the score tied, 5–5. The *Chicago Tribune* described the game's end: "Cronin started the fatal fourteenth with a double and Reynolds walked. Blue and Selph made a sterling pay to get Cronin at third and Blue flied to Rothrock. Then Berg picked on Lyons, one of the best pals he has in the world, with a single to left, scoring Reynolds and the game was over."

After delivering the winning blow, Berg rushed toward the Senators dugout with Lyons in pursuit. "I got to Moe in the locker room and began pushing him around," Lyons recounts. "He was doubled up with laughter. I gave him a couple of friendly punches. I said, 'Why'd you have to pick on me? You haven't had a hit in twenty years.' I told him he would have to pay for dinner that night."

Berg ignored off-season law practice in 1932 and departed for Japan with Lyons and O'Doul to instruct the Japanese collegians. After the instructional sessions, Lyons and O'Doul prepared to depart for America, while Moe remained in Japan.

Upon O'Doul's return to America he told newsmen, "As we were about to leave Tokyo for home an unusually large Japanese gentleman approached us on ship. Or we thought he was Japanese. He was in full kimono, wearing shoes mounted on wooden cleats. He also wore those traditional Japanese stockings separating each toe similar to a mitten. It was Moe. And he would only speak to us in Japanese."

Berg left Japan and traveled to Korea and China and then to India to converse with Sanskrit masters. He was depressed by the squalor of Calcutta and Bombay. He explored the Cambodian jungle and then moved on to Arabia to increase his knowledge of that tongue. He crossed into Palestine and traced the holy trails of Jerusalem, Bethlehem, and Nazareth. The conflicting green fields and sands of the Holy Land intrigued him. He then sailed to Athens to meet the linguistic scholars of Greece.

Berg's trip ended in Berlin in January of 1933 on the

day Hitler was appointed chancellor of the Reichstag. He returned to the United States convinced that the surging militarism and emotion inside Germany would end in war. *Christian Science Monitor* sports reporter Edwin Rumill recalls, "Moe would often visit the *Monitor* in those days and join us newsmen in discussing world events. He was emphatic that war would come. He was very positive about that."

In 1933 President Roosevelt shared the Washington limelight with the Senators. The team, comprised of players with excellent abilities but regarded as inferior to the Yankees, engineered a dramatic season to win the American League championship. The upset inspired enchanting baseball stories for years to come, a Broadway musical, and several Moe Berg vignettes.

In mid-season the Senators were fighting off the Yankees for the pennant. The team was playing the St. Louis Browns in oppressively humid Missouri weather, and Moe Berg was catching the second game of a doubleheader.

Berg's traditional Indian-colored face of summertime was sweating profusely in the fifth inning. His body poured water. After the third out he staggered to the Senators' bench declaring, "Gentlemen, I believe Satan's joined the team and I'm confident he's inside my uniform." Moe began taking off his uniform in the dugout as teammates doused him with water.

Luke Sewell, who caught the first game in victory, recalls, "It must have been a hundred and ten degrees that day and Moe hadn't been catching too much. And I believe Moe had to run the bases a few times during the game. Cronin waved me in from the bullpen, where I was trying to cool off from the first game. When I reached the dugout Moe was lying down on the bench. The heat was terrific and he was in pain.

"Moe said, 'Luke, I've done all I can. You'll have to come in. We have to win the pennant.'" Berg stretched out on the dugout floor advising, "I gotta rest the body, rest the body."

The Washington Senators won the American League pennant by seven games over Ruth, Gehrig, Lazzeri and the rest of the second-place Yankees. But the New York Giants defeated the Senators in the World Series, four games to one. Moe did not play. He remained in the bull-pen catching, hollering encouragement to his club, and advising pitchers what pitches to throw to batters when they went to the mound.

Sports columnist Shirley Povich of the *Washington Post*, recalls, "Moe never indicated to me any disappointment in not getting into the series. He was happy, I think, to have been part of a championship team. His momentum was victory always. He had his work cut out in the bullpen."

Luke Sewell, who did all the catching, gives his assessment: "Moe was too much of a gentleman, a team man, to complain. He'd do anything to win. Perhaps inwardly he felt hurt about not getting into a game, but he never expressed it to me. I'm sure Moe would have caught if it were a seven-game series. But we were fighting a losing battle with the Giants."

Cronin agrees that if the series had continued, Berg would have caught. "Moe was just as critical in the bull-pen. Losing the series in five games changed things."

American League statisticians noted at the end of the

1933 season that Moe had gone through four seasons with Chicago, Cleveland and Washington without making an error in one hundred and thirty-three games. The streak was broken at one hundred and thirty-seven games the following year.

Washington coach Al Schacht recalls vividly inserting Berg into the Senators' lineup during a crisis in the less romantic 1934 season:

"There would be no championship for the Senators in 1934. Our ballclub was shot. Cronin broke a wrist, Schulte broke a leg, several other ballplayers were wounded. We looked like a regiment that didn't do too well at the front. Anyway, we were shot down. Cronin's injury happened during the early part of September. Griffith then let Cronin go on his honeymoon. So I was made the manager and I was going to throw my brains all over the ball park.

"Because of all the injuries, I had to play our regular catcher, Sewell, in right field. We were breaking in a new young fellah by the name of Cliff Bolton. He had been with us for a year. So he catches a few games in Washington and then we go to Philadelphia for a series with the Athletics. Bolton comes to me in Philly and announces he broke his hand in the game yesterday. Now there's only a few of us left. The war is getting worse. Now, of course, there's only Moe Berg left to do the catching. It's batting practice time, I look around for Moe Berg, who is a very mysterious guy. I can't find him. It's getting close to game time. All of a sudden he comes to the park. And it's one of those Indian summer days, very hot. Moe hadn't caught in about six weeks and I don't think he's in the best of shape. I don't tell him about Bolton, just walk over and tell Moe he's going to catch today. I'm probably taking him away from a date with Plato in the bullpen, but we got problems. Whitehill is the pitcher and he's the kind of pitcher — why, one pitch would be down here and the next one up there. Poor Berg is going all over the lot to field the pitches. By the end of the fourth inning Moe looks like a punch-drunk fighter.

"Comes the seventh inning and Cramer comes to the plate for Philly. Now Cramer and Whitehill begin outstaring each other. Berg's down behind the plate waiting for something to happen and nothing happens. Cramer steps out of the box. Berg gets up and then Berg goes down. Then Whitehill walks off the mound. So Berg has got to get up again. The sun is blazing away. Now Whitehill returns from his walk and is on the mound again. Berg goes down. Cramer steps up to the plate, everybody is staring at everybody, and Cramer steps out of the box. Berg looks like an elevator and he's roaring mad. Whitehill and Cramer again go through their routine of trying to outmaneuver each other and suddenly Berg calls 'time.' Umpire Bill McGowan is behind the plate. McGowan calls time to find out what Berg wants. Now here's Berg showing his anger. He takes off his chest protector, takes his mask off, takes his shin guards off and piles everything on home plate. There's thousands in the ball park, remember. He turns to McGowan and says, 'I'll return when those two guys decide to play baseball. Right now I'm going to take a shower.' "

Schacht recalls also, "Once Moe asked me to do him a favor. Wanted me to take him to Princeton, where the two of us would give a baseball lecture to the athletes. First he wanted to go to his house in New Jersey to pick up some films he took on a trip around the world. Wanted the Princeton ballplayers to see these, too. I go to the house — he says I'm the first guy ever to be inside the house. So I walk in. God, he's got more newspapers in there than the *New York Times.* He warns me that they're alive and don't touch. 'When they're dead,' Moe says, 'I'll letcha have them.' Then I see a skeleton on the wall. I got scared. I said, 'Let's get out of here.' We get to the outskirts of Princeton and Berg all of a sudden said that he forgot the films and let's turn around and go back to the house. I said, 'My God, for a guy who's been to Princeton, Columbia, the Sorbonne and has eighty-five degrees you don't even know how to gather up films."

During the Princeton visit Berg told his audience, "Let me tell you what Schacht really thinks of me as an athlete. When I was catching with Cleveland and Schacht was in town with the Washington Senators he asked me to go out with him and drink a few beers. Now, Walter Johnson was manager of the Indians at the time and he was a stickler for training rules. So I said, 'Why Al, you know how Johnson is, everybody in by eleven-thirty.' But Schacht came back with 'Why, I'm sure Walter won't mind, Moe, as long as I don't keep any of the ballplayers out.' "

Washington also provided Berg with an outlet for his linguistic talents and for socializing with political dignitaries and the women that surrounded them. Upon completion of a ballgame, Moe often dined at various embassies. It was not uncommon for a tuxedo to hang in his locker.

Moe seldom failed to receive an invitation to social functions from Romance language–speaking countries. His reputation as a linguist, combined with his unlikely occupation, intrigued his hosts. Wearing white tie and tails, his rich black hair impeccably in place above a taut, athletic face, Moe garnered instant attention as he entered an embassy. He shook hands with diplomat friends and gracefully kissed the hands of women who approached him. His compliments to women were always in their native language. He disassociated himself from political discussion when waltz music commenced. He never tired of Strauss waltzes or the beautiful women whom he whirled across the floor. Despite his friendship with many newspaper reporters, he declined ever to speak to society writers covering functions.

Tommy Thomas, who was traded to the Senators from the White Sox, remembers, "In Washington Moe generally lived at the Wardman Park, never had to buy a meal as he dined at all the embassies where he talked their languages, and kissed the hands of more women than Valentino."

Berg was released by the Senators at the end of July 1934. Sports reporters and wire services speculated that he would retire to law or the classroom. Berg would do neither, for it was important that he be with a major league club at least for the remainder of the year. The all-star trip to Japan was ten weeks away.

Berg contacted his old friend Walter Johnson, the legendary pitcher and manager of the Cleveland Indians. Berg's conversation with Johnson was private but within seventy-two hours after his release from Washington, Berg was signed by the Indians. And he was welcomed for professional reasons as well as for whatever private reasons drove him to remain in the game.

The Indians had just lost the services of their regular catcher, Glenn Myatt, who had broken his ankle in a game with the Detroit Tigers days earlier.

The members of the 1934 all-star team, slated to play in Japan, had been chosen earlier in the year. The team did not include Moe Berg. Connie Mack had asked Berg to join the club and serve as its interpreter, as well as a player, but, for unknown reasons, he had rejected the offer. But in late August of 1934, when the Indians were in Boston for a series with the Red Sox, Moe received a telegram from Earl Mack, son of the Philadelphia manager, again asking him to join the tour. This time Moe Berg agreed.

Where Moe had gone after emerging from St. Luke's International Hospital with his panoramic film of Tokyo is not known. The course of its trip to military files in Washington is also a secret. Later that evening, when met by teammates, Moe brushed off curious inquiries. He suggested he missed the Omiya game because he didn't feel well. He discouraged any extensive probing of the matter. His excuse appeared lame to the players for two reasons. Moe Berg had a reputation for seldom being ill. Moreover, he had failed to inform Ruth, Mack or any ballplayer that he was sick. But an atmosphere of happiness characterized the trip, and little was made of the incident.

Several members of the all-star team and their wives recall that Moe Berg politely declined to accompany the group to social events during the stay in Japan.

Mrs. Lyon, whom Moe Berg ostensibly went to visit in

the hospital, recalls thirty-nine years later: "I really never saw Moe Berg. It was an extraordinary occurrence. Moe came with the pretext of visiting me. Despite heavy screening at the hospital he apparently said he had come to visit the ambassador's daughter, got on an elevator, and kept on going, somehow, to the hospital roof. Yes, I was his excuse. My daughter, Alice Emily's, birth was noted in Tokyo papers and that is where Moe most likely learned of it. St. Luke's was a very modern hospital and a skyscraper by Tokyo standards. I was on the sixth or seventh floor, I think. But Moe never entered my room. It was sometime later that I was first told of the incident. The pictures taken by Moe Berg at the hospital were used in the General Doolittle raid during the war."

Mrs. Lyon's husband, Cecil Burton Lyon, a career diplomat, said he had met Moe Berg in later years on one occasion but could not recall where it took place. Their daughter, now Mrs. Harry Thompson of New York City, was familiarized of the Tokyo filming by her parents. "I remember being told a long time ago of Moe Berg coming to the hospital and taking pictures that were later used during the war."

Charlie Gehringer, in recalling the trip, said, "I had heard years later that Moe had done something unusual, but he was extremely secretive. I really didn't realize that Moe was missing from the ballpark. Frank Hayes was doing most of the catching, I recall. I learned later that the pictures taken by Moe were so vital during World War II. We later felt Moe obviously had some direction to do what he did. He certainly didn't let on to anything. I didn't know how involved he was in things. I didn't have any

State Department letter from Secretary Hull and I didn't realize that Moe did. I know of no other players who took the trip that had one either. My other recollection of Moe on that trip is that of correcting some of the Japanese fellows on their grammar."

Lefty Gomez adds, "I remember Moe being missing from the ballpark that day. He had disappeared and no one on the team knew where the hell he was. Of course Moe was a mysterious guy all his life. He looked the same at six in the morning, eight in the evening or at midnight. He was always moving about. He was always coming from some place or other. No one ever knew where he lived or what he did with his time. He'd spend some time with the guys but overall Moe Berg was total mystery. You could expect anything as far as Moe was concerned. But being missing from the ballpark is something else again. He wasn't scheduled to catch that day but he should have been in uniform in the bullpen ready to warm pitchers up or play if necessary. But the game, of course, went on without Moe."

Mrs. June Gomez recalls, "I remember Moe did an awful lot of traveling in Japan. He took a lot of trips where other ballplayers and the rest of us did not go. We thought it unusual that Moe failed to take some of the scheduled socializing trips. He was always going off somewhere alone. But Moe was so pleasant on the trip and we all enjoyed him immensely. He was just different, that's all."

Pitcher Joe Cascarella was in the bullpen at Omiya during the game. He recalls, "Moe was missing from the park and the reason given those curious about his whereabouts

*

was 'physical indigence.' I don't believe anyone on the team was aware where Moe was during the game. Being quite close to Moe I wondered if he was all right and thought it strange that he hadn't informed anyone of his inability to play that day."

Cascarella remembers that Moe Berg "wasn't disposed" to discuss the matter with ballplayers other than to suggest casually he wasn't feeling well. "Moe's possession of the State Department letter was for reasons that are sufficiently obvious now. I know of no other member of the team that possessed one."

The pitcher adds, "Moe often went off by himself during the tour. And if I recall correctly I believe Moe had lost quite a bit of weight during the stay in Japan."

Cleveland Indians slugger Earl Averill remembers, "I always got along fine with Moe, I liked the man. We were teammates on the Cleveland Club when we went to Japan. It was a great trip. It wasn't until years later that I learned Moe was a spy. I didn't know it at the time. He was the right man, of course. Moe had the guts of a cat burglar. I remember Japanese authorities getting excited when our ship got too close to some island off Yokohama. It was some kind of fortification, I think. The ship was instructed to move away."

The consequence of the American visit for Matsutoro Shoriki, founder of the *Yomiuri* newspaper empire who contributed so significantly to the development of baseball in Japan, began while the tour was in progress. In their biography of Shoriki, authors Edward Uhlan and Dana L. Thomas wrote:

Shoriki was playing with dangerous emotions when he entered the baseball field, however. Young hot blooded "patriots," self-appointed patriots of the Japanese way of life, were on the loose. They missed nothing that appeared to them to be subversive.

In November of 1934, three young men of the "War God Society" visited Shoriki. The spokesman read Shoriki a letter of "accusation." It charged that Shoriki had "despoiled the sanctuary" of the stadium built as a memorial to the Emperor Meijii when he promoted a baseball game there between Japanese and American all-star teams. The presence of foreigners on sacred ground, the three youths charged, was a defilement. They also charged that the Hearst organization, with which Shoriki had close relations through International News Service, was anti-Japanese.

Three months later, on a cold February morning, Shoriki arrived for work early, as usual. As he stepped toward the gate of the Yomiuri Building he was stabbed viciously from behind. He shouted with surprise and pain and turned in time to see a man racing away, carrying a bloodied Japanese sword.

Blood gushed from the gaping wound in Shoriki's neck. As the street was deserted, Shoriki tried to make his way alone toward the Yomiuri dispensary. The foreman of the print shop saw him and rushed to his aid. Once in the dispensary Shoriki lost consciousness and was not revived for another five hours. He was kept in the hospital for fifty days and spent an additional month recuperating at a hot-spring rest resort.

Before leaving the United States for Japan Moe Berg had made reservations to return home via the Trans-Siberian Railroad.

He remained in Japan for two weeks after the conclusion of the all-star team visit. Moe then boarded the *Empress of Canada* for Shanghai, where he spent one day at the Hotel Grand, then flew to Peiping, where he remained for four days.

Train and plane travel brought Moe to Manchouli on New Year's Eve, 1934, for the start of the trip. At the time, he was one of the few Americans ever to ride the meandering Trans-Siberian tracks westward to their Moscow terminus. "I believe the American government was just as interested in my brother's observations in Siberia as it was in his Japanese mission," Dr. Berg theorizes.

The weather was thirty-five degrees below zero as the train began its seven-day, fifty-eight-hundred-mile journey. Moe moved from the untamed eastern environs of Siberia through miles of melancholy, snow-covered terrain. The train stopped at remote villages that hugged the tracks to unload passengers committed to harness the vast, untapped resources of no-man's-land. His camera, when opportunity allowed, filmed scenes and people as the celebrated train moved westward through Nakhodka, Khabarovsk, Chita, Irkutsk and Omsk. He took pictures throughout the trip, filming the rugged Ural Mountains. Subdued balalaika playing permeated the coach cars to lighten the journey, which ended in Moscow on January 6, 1935.

While Berg was in the Orient, Joe Cronin was sold by his father-in-law, Washington Senators owner Clark Griffith, to the Boston Red Sox at age twenty-seven for a hundred and twenty-five thousand dollars. Millionaire Red Sox manager Tom Yawkey immediately named Cronin team manager.

Yawkey gave the young manager absolute power over the destiny of the Red Sox. Cronin's first move was to bring Moe Berg, "if he can be found," to Boston.

Boston newspapers said the pact offered Moe for a player-coach position was the most lucrative the catcher had ever received in his baseball career. The amount was not disclosed. Berg accepted the job upon his return to the United States.

Berg loved Boston, its culture, architecture, and universities, its restaurants, which appealed to his gourmet tastes, its rare-book stores, its symphony and its excitement.

Berg would make the crucial decisions of his life in Boston, decisions that would lead to a dramatic impact on the nation as a whole. His reputation for being mysterious would soar. The Red Sox would also be his last ball team.

Boston rejuvenated Moe's baseball career, despite weary legs in their thirty-third year. He emerged from the bullpen to catch thirty-eight games and bat .286, delivering many key hits. "Moe lived up to every expectation," Cronin said of Berg's first year. His season, however, was discolored by the airplane death of humorist Will Rogers, who often joined Moe at World Series time. Rogers would generally greet his catcher friend by saying, "Moe, let's paint the town pink. Let's step out tonight with two exciting verbs." In reporting Rogers's accident, *New York World Telegram* sportswriter Tom Meany said, "Rogers' particular cronies were Moe Berg, the erudite catcher, who had flown some of the Siberian air routes which were Mr. Rogers' favorites, and Casey Stengel, the Dodger manager."

Yawkey believes that bringing Moe Berg to Boston was one of the finest moves ever made by the club:

"I was very close to Moe from the time he came to us. He had a tremendous impact on our players and I enjoyed

Moe pounces on the ball as the runner, blocked from view by the umpire, slides home. Moe was catching for the Red Sox in a game against the Cleveland Indians.

every darned minute with him. Each time the club was in New York we'd have dinner together at the Pierre, where I stayed. I would call Moe, but he would object, saying something like 'Tom, I'm only a ballplayer, you know.' And I would say, 'Moe, the deuce with that attitude, we're two people.' The thing was there has never been a man I enjoyed more, or got along with better in my lifetime than Moe Berg. His company was important to me.

"Moe would generally show up with a bunch of foreign

newspapers and I'd say, 'Moe, don't start talking Japanese
or Russian to me because I don't understand them.' We'd
talk about everything under the sun. And you'd walk away
from the man feeling great, no matter what your troubles.
He affected you that way. I got an insight on baseball from
Moe Berg. Few people knew the game better. There may
have been a few ballplayers who resented him because of
his education and wondered why he wasn't teaching languages instead of playing baseball. Moe was a very private
man basically. You might say he led two lives. A happy
man who loved baseball and a serious man who retreated
to other things when the game was over."

Cascarella, who joined the Red Sox in 1937, supports
the Yawkey philosophy of two Moe Bergs:

"Baseball for Moe, I believe, was a blessing as well as a
black shadow. His pride and curse. The game provided for
Moe certain intangibles that were advantageous. Baseball
gave him the opportunity of being on the playing field, in
the bullpen, on the bench and in the dugout with twenty-
five men, which, normally, he would not choose for himself. It gave him the good life. Meeting people, a livelihood, travel, a sense of really belonging. He had a very
unusual strain in him. He would have been far better off,
perhaps, if he wasn't so multitalented. If Moe could have
satisfied himself with a single pursuit — baseball, teaching,
or the law — there would have been less inner conflict. He
once said to me, 'Joe, I don't know what the hell I'm doing
in baseball year after year.' But Moe Berg would be on that
ball field the next day. He would be very meticulous about
getting ready for the game, and just as gung ho about
playing as anyone, and excited about being with the boys.

I believe that baseball derailed him from greater things. I think Moe Berg could have become a very, very important human being. Bigger than he became. . . .

"On our trip to Japan we stopped in Honolulu for a few days. When we got there he was speaking Japanese to some people. Moe had a remarkable ability to absorb sounds, like a Toscanini. He was a Toscanini of the mind. He was a Toscanini of thought and words. He was a great conductor.

"He had remarkable sensitivity, a real understanding of the breadth of things, and I think he had a pride and a wish that all human beings behave with a certain sense of grace. It hurt him, it irked him when people behaved in a fashion he thought was gross.

"Moe was a very kind man in the bullpen. He was a considerate catcher and coach. He would sit there and say to me, 'Joe, when you go in there you'll kill them. Break that curve ball off and keep the high, hard one inside.' He did this to alleviate any pangs of tension I may have had.

"The man had a tremendous sense of integrity and belonging to the club he was with. Under no circumstances would he give up. When they called Moe into a game he would run onto the ball field as if he were going to catch the first game of the World Series. Some of the fellows would chide his enthusiasm and say, 'Come on Moe, we're behind 7–1 and it's the eighth inning.' Moe would say something like, 'No, no, we can beat this club. A good rally will do it.' He just would not quit. And he wouldn't hesitate one minute to use words that weren't in the Bible. He would say that if that so and so knocks you down at the plate don't let him get away with it. His basic gentility could disappear fast if one of our hitters was knocked down. Moe Berg could get very, very excited. He was no Salvation Army lassie when it counted. But what I remember most about Moe is the warmth he generated on a ball club. No matter how poorly you performed, Moe would approach, say something kind, and you'd walk away ready to eat lobster."

"Broadway" Charlie Wagner was regarded as one of the most handsome men ever to wear a baseball uniform. His extravagant wardrobe belied a gentle nature and a burning desire to be a top major league pitcher. Wagner, now a Red Sox scout, recalls:

"I met Moe in spring training. I really was just a kid. I was still saying 'them horses' instead of 'those horses.' It offended Moe. He became my English teacher. He'd teach me in the bullpen. He'd take me to dinner and he became a great instrument in teaching me how to eat properly. He taught me all the little things that I think aided me later in life. If I sat before a meal Moe would say, 'You cut this way.' Once I was about to put a salad dish on my plate and he grabbed my hand explaining, 'Charlie, that's the waiter's job.' Consequently, as an athlete I was invited out to a lot of places to eat and talk. And the things Moe taught me worked out beautifully. I never felt out of place.

"One time I was on the brink of not making the club. We were finishing up spring training and scheduled to play the Cincinnati Reds. Cronin had said that I was either going to make the team or not on the strength of how I pitched that day. The realization of possibly being farmed out hurt. Moe came up to me and said, 'Charlie, I asked to catch you today.' I said, 'That's great, Moe. Thanks.' He emphasized, 'I just want you to follow my signs and do as I say. Believe in yourself, Charlie. You can do it.' He truly built up my confidence. Well, I pitched a three-hitter. I went the full nine innings and we beat the Reds 3–1.

"Moe rushed out and hugged me saying, 'Charles, let's go north; we're in.' The man had me in his power and I confess I enjoyed every moment. He used to say he had to rest the body, rest the body. But he really tested its durability. He'd get up and say, 'Charlie, what the hell are you going to learn in bed?'

"The aura surrounding Moe just never seemed to let up. Once he murmured something about having to see President Roosevelt and left. You wondered, because you associated Moe with being a ballplayer. Then we opened the season in Washington and President Roosevelt is wheeled into the stadium and when seated waves to Moe. Jim Farley was with the President and Moe brought me over for an introduction."

Farley, postmaster general in the Roosevelt administration and long one of the Democratic Party's most influential men, mingled with the catcher at Washington affairs. Farley recalls, "I enjoyed Moe and admired his intellectuality. There was an air of great confidence surrounding the man, although he was by no means a snobbish person. He was one of the most memorable persons I ever met and certainly baseball's most unusual personality."

Recalling Moe's range of friends, Wagner continued his reminiscences:

"His priority for the day might involve getting the son of a waiter into Princeton or dining with celebrities.

"I remember Moe taking me into Lindy's one evening

for dinner with Oscar Levant and John Kieran of the
Times. Oscar was a great baseball fan and he and Moe
would argue baseball, with Levant wanting to know why
the Red Sox were losing and the Yankees winning. Moe
would put the problem in proper perspective as Oscar
drank his twentieth cup of coffee and blew cigarette smoke
in all directions. We talked baseball and ate in a smoke
screen. Moe was a great eater, always dining with a black
suit on. I never went into my pockets. He wouldn't let you
pay.

"I only saw Moe angry twice. If someone touched his
live newspapers he would be furious. Once on a train a
ballplayer told Moe he didn't believe he had really ab-
sorbed some of the dead papers he had just discarded. A
crowd surrounded the pair and looked at the papers as
Moe virtually recited word for word every major story.

"The second time I saw Moe upset was when he had a
small sty on his eye. Always in perfect health he thought
this was awful and didn't want anyone near him. It em-
barrassed him. I never saw Moe have a cold.

"Moe was a good catcher. One of his tricks — he used it
only on Ladies' Day — came while catching a pop fly foul
ball behind home plate. He'd throw the mask in the air,
catch the ball and then catch the mask with the other
hand. He would drive me crazy.

"I remember Dom DiMaggio coming to me when he
joined the club. He had just met Moe for the first time and
was curious about him. Dom said he entered a room and
saw Moe attired in a Japanese kimono. DiMaggio said Moe
was in bed in between a thousand newspapers and had a
straw hat on his head. I told Dom never to be surprised

when he saw Moe moving about in a kimono. He often wore it. His surprises never ceased. The advice from Moe that I remember mostly was, 'Charlie, don't be just a ballplayer. Be a gentleman. It's important and it's right.' "

Dominic DiMaggio, the third member of baseball's most famous playing family to make the major leagues, recalls:

"Not too long after I joined the Red Sox I had occasion to room with Moe Berg. I think he was my first roommate. Soon afterward I injured an ankle and was confined to my room. After a few days I had a number of visitors. Moe, of course, was a great linguist and had all kinds of foreign papers scattered throughout the room, which wasn't large. Moe kept all the papers in neat stacks. One stack was Japanese, one Italian, another Portuguese and so on. The stacks used to grow as he tried to read them all between ball games. He used all the furniture in the place for the papers. They covered every chair. And people who came to visit me would respect the papers and stand. But one day Manager Cronin came — he had been to the room before and always respected the papers — and couldn't find a place to sit down. He was kind of tired and more as a practical joke than anything else Cronin took a stack of Greek papers and mixed them with some other tongue. Cronin said, 'I'm entitled to sit on a chair just as much as Berg's newspapers.' I knew, of course, that one of the great sins had been committed.

"After a few hours I went downstairs for something to eat. When I returned I found everything had been cleared out of the room, the foreign newspapers, Berg's clothes, everything. But Moe left me a note, saying, 'Dominic, you're much too popular and have too many visitors. My newspapers are too valuable to me.'

"I accepted his concern and the next time I saw him I said, 'I understand Moe.'"

Berg's first four years with the Red Sox, 1935 through 1938, saw him in approximately thirty-eight games each season, sometimes to catch only a few innings. He was reasonably productive, with ninety-six hits in three hundred and sixty-four times at bat for a .259 average. He was now thirty-six years old.

Late in the 1936 season, as the Yankees headed toward easy capture of the American League pennant, with a hundred and two victories under Manager Joe McCarthy, an extraordinary incident occurred at Yankee Stadium.

The Yankees were on the field for pregame practice, while their opponents, the Red Sox, waited for their practice turn in the visitors' dugout. Yankee infielders Tony Lazzeri, Frank Crosetti, and Red Rolfe scooped up practice grounders and fired the ball to Lou Gehrig at first base. Catcher Bill Dickey rushed in front of home plate for hypothetical bunts and rifled the ball to first, second and third bases. Outfielders George Selkirk, Joe DiMaggio, and Jake Powell raced their famous legs to catch fly balls hit by coaches. Thousands of fans sat watching the players. In the Yankee bullpen, Lefty Gomez, on his way to thirteen victories and seven losses for the season, was warming up. Curve balls, fast balls, the baffling sinker balls.

A sole Red Sox player moved slowly across the outfield toward the Yankee bullpen. It was Moe Berg. He looked toward Gomez and, as the left-hander finished his warm-up, approached him.

"Lefty, do you have a minute?" asked Moe Berg.

Gomez recalls, "I said, 'Hello, Moe, how's things?' Moe

began talking about the trip to Japan of two years earlier. He was interested in what pictures I had taken during the tour. He was particularly interested in any pictures I had taken of Yokohama Harbor, and asked if I had any of Shanghai and Hong Kong. I didn't know what the devil he was driving at.

"We continued to talk about the trip and the filming. During the Japanese tour June and I took a lot of pictures with our motion picture camera. We did this in Yokohama, Tokyo, Osaka and Hokkaido. And during our trip around the world we took pictures of other places in the Orient. I told Moe this — he had seen us take some in Japan. In Hokkaido Japanese officials took my camera away. I believe they took a camera away from Moe, too. I got my camera back later. Well, we continued to talk for a while and then Moe made a request. He said it was important. He gave me an address in Washington and asked me if I would send my pictures there. I believe it was a government address, if I remember right. Moe said, 'I guarantee you, Lefty, that the pictures will be sent back to you.' I mailed the film to Washington. I don't know specifically who received them. They kept it for seven or eight months and then it was returned with a letter that expressed thanks. I never mentioned the incident. My camera was a sixteen-millimeter Stewart Warner and it could film for quite a distance if it was set for it."

During 1936 Japan was increasing its military strength, and militarists were gaining political clout. The nation had shown only slight economic improvement over the more depressing period of the early 1930s, but its population was continuing to soar and the panacea appeared to be another thrust into North China. This would come the following year as the peaceful views of many Japanese were overshadowed by the uncompromising military. Further, Japan looked to Germany, whose authoritarian government was congenial and responsive to pleas for friendship, aid and military treaties. Japan allied with Germany against Russia by signing the Anti-Comintern Pact, which stipulated that if Russia attacked either of the signatories it would be construed as an attack against both nations.

America watched the growing international crisis while mired in its historic depression. The nation, however, was not completely dormant. Its military apparatus accepted surveillance of its potential enemies whenever it could be provided — even on the ball field.

Despite the militancy of the Japanese government, Moe's love and respect of the Japanese people remained undiminished. He stayed in close contact with many Japanese friends. One of them, Takizo Matsumoto, whom he had met in Tokyo in 1932, had expressed a wish to come to the United States and study for his master's degree at Harvard.

In a letter to Moe from Fresno, California, dated January 7, 1937, Matsumoto tells of his hope and determination:

My Dear Moe:
Picked up my pen twice before to write to you. Just returned from another trip. The Japanese football team was here and played against the Los Angeles All-Stars. Although the lighter Japanese team was defeated 19 to 6, their debut here was more than satisfactory. In fact, the midget Japanese team surprised everyone, including their own coach. Being

responsible for starting football in Japan I was called upon then to help them struggle through some of the difficulties they were forced to face. The team left for Japan this noon and I am again relieved to have my own time.

Your booklets, wire and air mail all reached me. I sent everything to Dean Lombard [George Lombard, then assistant dean of the Harvard Business School]. I expect to hear from him any minute now. I will be called away for a week to Los Angeles on business (lecture). I will return to Fresno again and leave for Boston around the 23rd, that is, if I am given admission. I hope everything will be O.K. I am going to have some difficulties with the yen from Japan for it won't be near enough to cover all of my expenses. I am racking my brains to make both ends meet. At all hazard, I am determined to stay at Harvard until June next year and receive my M.A. I shall never stop thanking you for everything you have done and will do for me. I'll be right up in Japan as soon as I return with my degree. I'll make you proud of me yet. Where can I meet you? Where are you going to play baseball? Are you going to play for Boston this year? Let me hear from you again before I leave Fresno. Am dying to see you.

Brotherly yours,
"Taki" Frank Matsumoto

Moe brought Matsumoto to Harvard to assist in the enrollment effort.

Harvard Business School dean George Lombard recalls, "I remember Moe Berg bringing Matsumoto to Harvard. I was an assistant dean of the Business School at the time. I believe it was another assistant dean, John Fox, who helped with Matsumoto's enrollment. Matsumoto was enrolled in February of 1937 and received his master's degree in business administration in June of 1938."

In 1938, Moe discarded his basic rule of keeping his

intellectual life private when he agreed to appear on "Information Please," a popular radio program of that era that asked largely esoteric questions pertaining to all fields of human endeavor. Berg had been induced to go on the show by baseball officials who wanted to erase the general notion that ballplayers were a bunch of "dese" and "dem" guys. Moe startled hundreds of thousands of listeners by his commanding knowledge. More than ten thousand persons called the National Broadcasting Company, the program's producer, demanding to know more about Moe Berg.

Among Moe's correct answers were that "loy" is the ancient French word for "law"; the Willie-Nicky exchange were pre–World War telegrams between the czar and the kaiser; that the Bordereau letter convicted France's innocent Captain Alfred Dreyfus of espionage; Halley's Comet of 1910 is the brightest comet; Venus is the brightest planet we see; and that poi is the Hawaiian substitute for bread.

Dan Golenpaul, ex-editor of *Information Please Almanac*, was even more intrigued by Moe Berg away from his program: "I had a nice relationship with Moe but I knew nothing about him. No one else did either. He sort of withdrew — there was an untouchable quality in his makeup. He was the man who wouldn't talk."

H. G. Salinger of the *Detroit News* attempted to find a hole in Berg's knowledge by joining forces with a group of writers. In the wake of the "Information Please" success, Berg was tiring of the publicity surrounding his appearances and agreed to one last confrontation with questions. Salinger's column on the last appearance refers to Berg as a man "who has more degrees than a majority of the college professors and more learning. He is a master mathematician and linguist, proficient in ancient and modern languages and reads, speaks and writes more than a dozen of them. When he was invited to appear on the Information Please radio program he flabbergasted the intellectuals with the breadth and depth of his knowledge. He astonished even those who know him well. Since there are few things more pleasurable to the average human being than proving an expert wrong we asked Professor Berg whether he would answer a number of questions carefully prepared in the hope of stumping him. He said he would try.

"Who or what are the Seven Sleepers, the Seven Wise Masters, the Seven Wise Men, the Seven Wonders of the World and the Seven Stars?"

Professor Berg answered the first question: "The Seven Sleepers, according to legend, were seven youths of Ephesus that the Emperor Decius ordered imprisoned in a cave. They slept in the cave for nearly two hundred years."

The Seven Wise Masters? "It is the title of a collection of ancient Oriental tales. They concern the son of a king who was taught by seven wise masters. He studied the stars and discovered himself in danger of death if he spoke within seven days. His life is saved each day by one of the seven masters. At the end of the seven-day speechless period he saved himself."

"So far so good, now who are the Seven Wise Men?"

"They are known as the Seven Sages of Greece, I think," said Professor Berg. "They were Periander of Corinth, Pittacus of Mitylene, Thales of Miketus, Solon of Athens,

Bias of Priene, Chilo of Sparta and Cleobulus of Lindus."

The Seven Wonders of the World?

"They are seven monuments — the pyramids of Egypt, the walls and hanging gardens of Babylon, the Temple of Diana at Ephesus, the statue of the Olympian Jupiter at Athens, the Mausoleum at Halicarnassus, the Colossus of Rhodes, and the Pharos, or lighthouse, of Alexandria."

"What about Niagara Falls and the Grand Canyon?" we asked.

"Neither is a monument," answered Professor Berg. "The Seven Wonders of the World were identified before Niagara Falls and the Grand Canyon were discovered."

"As to the Seven Stars, Professor?"

"You probably refer to Pleiades, or Pleiads, a group of stars in the constellation of Taurus the Bull, but they are so close together it is impossible to count them with the naked eye."

"Still hoping to stump Prof. Berg, the next question was, who were the Black Napoleon and the Modern Hannibal?"

The answer: "Dessalines, who drove the French out of Haiti and founded the republic, was, and still is, known as the Black Napoleon. General Cornwallis was nicknamed the Modern Hannibal by General Greene of the American forces. He is still called General Cornwallis."

"Who was Poppea Sabina?"

"A notorious Roman beauty of 50 A.D. Nero married her and later had her executed, just like that."

"Well, then, who was Calamity Jane?"

"Her real name was Jane Burke. She was an Indian scout like Buffalo Bill. She was aide to General Custer and

General Miles. Later she carried the mail between Deadwood, South Dakota, and Custer, Montana."

Subsequent news stories of the inability to trip up Berg appeared in hundreds of newspapers across the country. Thousands of letters poured into Fenway Park over the next six months. Moe did not open them, confiding to friends that he felt he had made a serious mistake. His concern was fortified as hundreds of fans flocked around the bullpen. They hurled challenges and questions at Berg. "Moe, recite the Book of Leviticus!" "Moe, is it walruses or walrii for the plural?" "Moe, what color were Martha's bloomers at the inauguration?" A livid Moe threw baseballs back to laughing pitchers.

One of the "Information Please" regulars was *New York Times* columnist John Kieran, who wrote often of Moe during the years leading up to World War II. Commenting in *This Week* magazine, Kieran said: "As a Princeton alumnus he was naturally interested in the annual Princeton and Yale football disputes. Moe and I made a date to ride down to Princeton on a train from New York. Being well acquainted with his taste for literature I brought a book along. It was an old, thick, dog-eared Latin dictionary. During the train ride we poured over the quotations from Caesar, Cicero, Virgil and Horace. We traced words through their gradual change in spelling and meaning from the original Latin and French into English. We grubbed among the roots of the Romance languages. Just as the football special arrived at Princeton Junction, Moe looked up and said, 'John imagine wasting time and money in a nightclub when you can have fun like this.'"

Reflecting on his friend years later, Kieran adds:

"Moe was one of the purest scholars I have known; certainly the most scholarly athlete ever. He learned because he loved to learn. It was his principal momentum in life.

"Moe wasted his time in baseball, I believe. He could have become a Supreme Court justice with that rare brain he possessed. And a damn sight better than some we've had. He could have been a Brandeis. But, Moe was a sybarite. He enjoyed baseball, yes, but he wanted the best life — the best food, the opportunity to travel, meet the most interesting people, read the best books.

"And being a sybarite, I believe, is why Moe never got married. He didn't want anything to interfere with these intellectual pursuits. That was his greatest joy and learning was the greatest playfield for his brain. Baseball gave him his entree for this life. Yet the joy was that Moe wouldn't bother with a nitwit if he had ten million dollars, but a poor fellow with a good brain — Moe was all ready for him.

"I remember Moe and I flying back from a World Series game in Detroit. He was trying to give me a brief course in Japanese or Chinese, I don't remember which. Whether up in the clouds or on the ground he was Moe Berg. I'm glad I met him, rest the body, rest the body."

In response to published or private suggestions that he devote his energies to another field, Berg's answer never varied: "I'd rather be a ballplayer than a president of a bank or a justice on the United States Supreme Court."

Ralph McGill, who was a sports writer before he became editor of the *Atlanta Constitution*, had been intrigued by Berg after a humorous spring training incident during the 1933 season.

"It seems this particular ballplayer with the Washington ball club was not feeling so well," McGill wrote in a column on April 11, 1937.

" 'What's the matter?' asked Moe Berg.

" 'I don't know. I feel a lot of aches and pains,' said the ballplayer.

" 'Maybe you are suffering from intestinal fortitude,' said Moe Berg.

" 'What's that?'

" 'It's something like the influenza.'

" 'Hey, maybe that's what I got. Intestinal fortitude, eh? What do you do for intestinal fortitude?'

" 'You take aspirin,' said Moe Berg.

"The next morning the player came down from his room at the hotel. He spied Moe Berg.

" 'Moe,' he said, 'You ought to be a doctor. You cured my intestinal fortitude in one night with that aspirin stuff.'

"Ever since I heard that story I've wanted to meet Moe Berg. Yesterday I did. He's in town with the Red Sox.

"In many ways he is one of the most remarkable men in baseball. He came right out of the Ivy League, leaving the cloistered halls of Princeton in 1923 to join, of all clubs, the Brooklyns. He's one of the few players to belie the ancient and accepted axiom: 'Once a Dodger always a Dodger.'

"He isn't. He's still Moe Berg.

"Somehow, I got the impression that Moe Berg gets a lot of drive out of this thing called life. Which is as it should be."

Ted Lyons, a Baylor University graduate and one of the game's most erudite players, always chastized his friend for failing to write during the off-season:

Vinton, La.
December 9, 1937

Dere Moburg:—

Ef ye ainta gonta anster mie letter thin ye're gettin a ballin out C. Whin a felluh putts hisself out two rite thrie er fore paiges too un knowcount lauyer well he can at lease uxpect a replie in dew time ucordin to yer books.

Jess fer that Ima gonna go on and cover this paige with no news of konsequensas. Ye've probabblie got back in the big town and put on one o them rackoon koats an coledge equipments an a trying to maik folks think ye're still in Princetown but I shoulduva spelt Prince diffunt on account of ye aint ackted rite about keepin in tuch with yer — frens????? Git yer head outa them books an maibe ye culd call fer the rite pitch wunce in a while. Guldness nose ye sertantly wurked about five years offin me by a callin curv, curv, curv and curv an a gettin me in jam after jam which was hard to extrikate wonsself from, and besids a warin out the arms uv all hour pichers an account o ue knowed ye wuz a gonta be all over the leeg and laff at how ye wore the wite Socks arrums out er sumpin. Ye've got the repputashion o bein in telagent, huh, an having degrees frum coledges wich i dont theenk is sow cause the only way ye cud have degrees is to ketch fever er flu er sumpin an ef my vote kounts fer anithing ye dont no nuthin. Always a spouttin off like ye knowed Franch, Spinach, Attalian er sum langage whin ye dont eaven no ignlish. I member a time whin ye ast a Spanyard the way two the ballpark and he didunt no whutinhell ye wuzza talkin bout. Now dunnie that ef ye kan. Ef ye wanna reform an try an rite a sampple o yer inglish I may rite ye sum knews presentlie. In the meantime why dont ye jess udmitt ye doan no nuthin an rite me it.

A fren????? Oh yeh

One of his favorite studies was astronomy. On one occasion when the Red Sox were in Philadelphia, Moe brought teammates on a tour of the famed Fels Planetarium of the Franklin Institute. Astronomer I. M. Levitt, director of the planetarium from 1949 till 1971, recalls his first encounter with Berg:

"I believe it was in 1937 while I was assistant director of the planetarium. I had just finished a lecture and everyone had left the room but this tall, handsome man who kept asking questions about the constellations. I asked him who he was and he said, 'You probably don't know me. I'm Moe Berg.' Well, of course, I had heard of him. I was a

semipro baseball player in Philadelphia and a fan of the
game. I got to know Moe real well. He was one of the most
inquisitive persons I've ever met. He would ask questions
about the origins of the legends of mythology. I had the
feeling he knew more than I did. He was well versed in the
legends. Sometimes he would come over to the planetarium at night. My wife, Alice, and I and Moe would stay
up till one or one-thirty in the morning using the big
telescope at the institute for observing the sky. I would
point out things on the moon and the planets. Moe would
ask about the conditions on the planets. He was perfectly
qualified to give a lecture on the constellations. I thought
it would be a terrific idea if he would give a lecture and I
asked him to. He accepted the invitation, but then at the
last minute, decided against it. I think he got stage fright."

Stories of Moe Berg's bullpen life continued in profusion.

Cronin brought Al Schacht to the Red Sox as a coach.
Pitcher Rube Walberg was hurling for the Red Sox in a
mid-season game and being pounded by opposition batters.

"Cronin was on the bench that day because of a leg
injury," Schacht recalls. "Cronin says to me, 'Al, get Jack
Wilson in to pitch. Walberg's having a rough time.' Jack
Wilson was a relief pitcher in the bullpen and always had a
front seat for Berg's stories. I said to Cronin, 'Joe, there's
no way we can get Wilson to the mound.' Cronin replied,
'We can't get Wilson into the game? What do you mean
we can't get him — he's still with the ball club, isn't he?' I
said, 'Yes, Joe, but Moe Berg has him somewhere in Russia
and he can't leave the place without a passport. And he
doesn't have one.' "

Donald Davidson, a high school student, was bat boy for the Red Sox while Berg served in the bullpen. Davidson, now a vice-president of the Atlanta Braves, recalled being helped academically by Moe.

In his book *Caught Short* Davidson wrote, "I was puzzled by English, not to mention Latin and French, so Moe volunteered to help me. Boston pitching dictated how much schoolwork we did during a game. When a pitcher went the route, Moe did not have to catch in the bullpen and we hit the books. Joe Cronin, then the Bosox manager and later longtime president of the American League, noticed that Berg and I had books in the bullpen. When Moe explained to the manager what he was doing, Cronin needled him. 'Moe,' said Joe, 'our pitching would be vastly improved if you devoted more time to catching in the bullpen and less time to Don Davidson's lessons.' I always amazed my parents when I brought my report card home — A in Latin and A in French."

Moe Berg enjoyed poetry, and Edgar Allan Poe was his favorite poet. *Christian Science Monitor* sportswriter Edwin Rumill recalls being with Moe in Baltimore, where Poe is buried in the small Westminster graveyard, in the mid-1930s.

"Moe asked me to join him in a visit to Poe's grave. He was quite excited by the impending visit and on the way to the grave Moe related his affection for Poe and his work. We entered the small graveyard behind a church and went to Poe's grave. We stood there and Moe continued to discuss Poe's work emphatically. Then, all at once, standing in his black suit beside the gravestone Moe recited:

Once, upon a midnight dreary, while I pondered, weak
  and weary,
Over many a quaint and curious volume of forgotten lore,
While I nodded, nearly napping, suddenly there came a
  tapping,
As of someone gently rapping, rapping at my chamber
  door.
" 'Tis some visitor," I muttered, "tapping at my chamber
  door —
Only this and nothing more."

"Moe recited the entire poem and then we left," said
Rumill. In fact, Berg could recite all of Poe's poems.

In 1939 Moe entered his fifteenth year in the major
leagues. His foremost disappointment throughout his baseball years continued: his father still refused to see him play
professionally. Moe told baseball friends that his greatest
joy would be to see his father in the stands, a joy far
greater than breaking Babe Ruth's home-run record. "No
matter how much I entreat the man, my father will not see
me play. Perhaps he's to be commended. He's a great man
who sticks by his convictions."

Dr. Berg recalls, "Our father believed Moe's pursuits
should be elsewhere. He wanted Moe to devote his mind
and energies to a profession; total commitment to law or
teaching languages in a university. I remember during the
depression standing outside the pharmacy talking with my
father. We were discussing income and how difficult it was
for everybody in the country. And then we referred to
Moe.

"I said, 'Well look, Pa, after all Moe's making a living. He's a baseball player.'

"And my father said, 'A sport,' then turned his head and feigned spitting. He did not like it.

"When Moe got his law degree he didn't want to put it to practical use. He was with a prestigious law firm on Wall Street in the off-season but the practical side of law didn't appeal to him. Theoretically the law was good. I guess when he saw the shenanigans involved in being a successful lawyer he gave up."

Dr. Berg adds that while his father remained implacable on the family baseball conflict, "My mother would go to see Moe play against the Yankees every once in a while. Like any mother she was proud to see her son's name in the newspapers."

Moe seldom missed the annual Hall of Fame game at Cooperstown, New York. Arthur Daley, Pulitzer Prize–winning sports reporter for the *New York Times*, years later recalled the opening Hall of Fame game in 1939:

"There was a special train that ran from New York City to Cooperstown. On the way home I found myself sitting beside Moe Berg, whom I had heard so much about but had never met. We were talking away and then — using a word that I had written but never pronounced — I said, 'Then the player hit the ball off the facard.' And Moe, in that soft voice of his, said, 'Arthur, it's facade, facade, with a soft c.' Moe then instructed that it came from a Romance language background and proceeded to give me the philology of the word back to the ancient Latin. I've never forgotten that and I don't believe I ever used the word again.

"As the years went along we gravitated toward each other. I guess I felt as close to Moe as anyone in baseball. When you get a pure intellectual who loved the game the way Moe did, you felt, well, the game isn't entirely kid stuff. I admired and respected Moe and once I asked him why he remained in the game so long and why he was so fiercely devoted to it. And Moe said, 'Why Arthur, it's my theater, it's my theater.' "

Despite the declining number of Moe's playing days he continued to command press attention. Foreign periodicals frequently wrote about him. Linguistic scholars and statesmen were particularly curious.

As the military situation in Europe worsened in the fall of 1938, Anthony Eden of Britain, a linguist as well as a statesman, arrived in the United States to deliver a political address. Before his talk he met in his Waldorf Astoria suite with Moe Berg. The *Philadelphia Evening Bulletin*'s "Sports Parade" column reported on December 17: "The other night in New York while thousands waited to hear Anthony Eden, former British Foreign Minister, talk on foreign affairs, the dapper British diplomat, shortly after his arrival, was chatting with a baseball player. The player was Morris Berg, otherwise Moe, a graduate of Princeton who later studied at the Sorbonne in Paris. While Mr. Eden adjusted his white tie, Moe lounged in a chair in his room discussing certain Sanskrit verb forms."

Murray Robinson, sports editor of the *Newark Star Eagle* wrote: "Moe lightens the travel-bred boredom of Boston scribes by naming the towns whence perfect strangers hail, whether they be Americans, Frenchmen, Basques, or what-not. Moe is one of the few baseball players who attends all World Series games religiously and at the recent series in Cincinnati he furnished startling evidence of his unerring instinct and sharp ear for the vagaries of inflection and lingo. Passing by a taxi parked near the hotel, he cocked an attentive ear towards the cabbie, who was talking to someone else.

" 'That fellow,' said Moe, 'comes from Kansas, somewhere near Coffeyville.' The cynics scoffed—but one of them asked the driver — and sure enough, the man was born not near Coffeyville, but right in it!

"Then a Boston newspaperman told another story.

"The Red Sox were in New York and he and Berg were walking into their hotel one evening when Moe's attention was attracted by a commotion in the revolving door. A distinguished-looking old gentleman with a red face and a white mustache was stuck in the contraption and growling in a deep, heart-felt basso profundo.

" 'That gent,' announced Berg, 'is a Frenchman from Marseille.' He went to the old gentleman's rescue, extricated him from his relentless trap, while speaking to him in French. The stranger was profuse in his thanks. He spoke English and soon verified, for the benefit of the gaping scribes, that he was indeed from Marseille."

1939 turned out to be Berg's last playing season. That year the Red Sox unveiled rookie outfielder Ted Williams. Two weeks after Williams joined the club, sportswriters asked Moe to assess the young player.

"He'll be great," Moe said. "For one thing he asks more sensible questions than most kids coming up. He's always eager to learn something. A little while ago he asked me what Red Ruffing will throw with two strikes and no balls on a left-handed batter and was curious as to how Ruffing's fast ball breaks. That demonstrates he is interested in making it and willing to learn. If he's no Joe DiMaggio in the field he's still a capable outfielder."

Williams remembers his rookie-season impression of Berg: "I kept looking at this man. He must have been about thirty-six or so and I was just a kid. And I kept saying to myself, 'Is this Berg guy some kind of an act, or what?' I watched him and watched him, listened to him, and his special uniqueness never faded. I concluded it wasn't an act but here was some kind of different human being. Hell, I never saw a show like that and Moe never knew he was performing. That was the beauty of it. Moe couldn't hit much in his last years and when he got a hit it was a big event. I remember Moe rammed one ball pretty good off the left-field wall and when he got back to the bench he said something like, 'That's the way you're supposed to hit them, Ted. I hope you were watching.' Moe was absolutely unique in baseball. He was something to remember and he certainly had a real man's guts."

On Sunday mornings in Boston, the ancient Cathedral of the Holy Cross has welcomed decades of communicants into its vast, solemn interior for mass. Priests before Vatican II rendered praise unto the Lord in stately Latin as churchgoers followed its English translation in their missals. Moe often sat through these Sunday masses to enjoy the Latin that never permeated the bullpen or almost any other residence in the twentieth century. Richard Cardinal Cushing, then auxiliary bishop of the Boston archdiocese, was a baseball fan and a friend of Moe Berg. On his visits to Fenway Park the cardinal told Moe that his church believed in miracles but he wasn't confident it could generate one to assist his hitting. The pair would discuss Latin before game time.

"Moe's appearance at mass was a unique and beautiful occurrence when you consider he was out of the faith," recalled Monsignor John Dillon Day of St. Mary's of the Hills Church, Milton, Massachusetts, a baseball enthusiast and noted linguist. "Moe's deep love of language and scholarship brought him to the cathedral."

During Berg's last playing year, Richard McCann wrote in *This Week* magazine of him: "He is father confessor to teammates in trouble and big brother to bewildered rookies. He took the blame for a midnight escapade one training season to save one player's scalp and acted as a body guard and shield for another buddy when an irate gentleman was seeking to wreak considerable damage on the lad."

Moe's Red Sox teammates recall a player who had a serious drinking problem. The player asked Moe if he could room with him for a few days. Moe agreed despite his penchant for living alone. Players as well as management seldom knew where Moe resided. He often moved from one apartment to another.

Twenty minutes before a game at Fenway Park, the imbibing player was not in uniform. Moe commanded two pitchers to join him in a search for the athlete. The trio rushed out of Fenway Park in uniform, startling thousands of persons on their way to the game as they ran to the Myles Standish Hotel, about four blocks from the park.

Entering Berg's room they found the missing player sprawled on the floor, Moe's foreign newspapers serving as a meandering mattress and pillow.

Moe's generally subdued voice increased several octaves as he asked, "Oh, Lord, where have I offended thee? Those papers were alive."

When they returned to the ball park without the missing athlete, players asked Moe if their teammate was all right.

"He's devastated," Berg muttered. "And so are France, Spain and England."

Moe Berg's newspaper addiction reached curious proportions in Detroit as the Red Sox took on the Tigers. An incident in the dugout led to a subsequent *New York Times* advertisement. It read:

"The question of what ballplayers do in the winter falls into the same general classification as 'What happens to your lap when you stand up?' But our John Kieran has given us a good tip.

"For at least part of every day, winter and summer — says Mr. Kieran — Coach Moe Berg of the Red Sox reads the *New York Times*.

"One day when the Red Sox were playing in Detroit, Berg's *Times* arrived late. And Manager Cronin was astonished during a hot third inning to find ensconced in the team's dugout, the boy who brought Moe's paper!

"Moe Berg — ballplayer, lawyer, alumnus of three universities — is typical of *Times* readers in his feeling that nothing else can take the place of the *Times*."

The advertisement was accompanied by a cartoon depicting the Red Sox dugout, players sitting along an extended bench, except for one space, which was "reserved" for Moe Berg's newsboy.

In the days that followed the advertisement hundreds of fans tried to pass newspapers from various cities into the bullpen, where ushers and Berg kindly waved them off.

Moe spent most of the 1939 season, his last as an active player, in the bullpen. He caught only fourteen times that year, in which the Red Sox finished in second place, seventeen games behind the Yankees.

On the few occasions that he was called from the bullpen to catch, Moe would run to the Red Sox dugout to put on his catcher's equipment. Players on the bench would applaud the rare sight. Then, speaking confidentially low and feigning he had forgotten the rules, he'd ask, "Gentlemen, does everyone still get three strikes out there?"

Moe played the last game of his career on August 30 against the Detroit Tigers in Briggs Stadium in Detroit. In the fourth inning Ted Williams and Jim Tabor hit back-to-back home runs off Freddie Hutchinson. Moe stepped up to the plate and slammed the second pitch into the left-field stands for his sixth major league home run, giving the Red Sox a temporary lead of 6–2 as the bench burst into cheers for their bullpen ace. The home run drove Hutchinson from the mound. Detroit rallied to win the game, however, 7–6. Berg ended the season with nine hits in thirty-three times at bat for a .273 batting average and a lifetime major league mark of .243. He had played in 663 games.

Baseball began to pall on Moe as Europe became embroiled in war. Nazi Germany, its domestic, political and religious terror unparalleled since the Inquisition, moved its armies into Poland on September 1, 1939. Two days later Great Britain, aware of Hitler's implacability and fearful of invasion, declared war on the Third Reich. Only the brilliance of the Royal Air Force kept the great German war machine in check as German generals slaughtered to victories in other lands.

The Wehrmacht generated invincibility. In the background German scientists, considered the world's most brilliant, attempted to produce the atomic bomb, which would assure world conquest. Albert Einstein, who had fled Germany and become the head of the Institute for Advanced Studies at Princeton, sent a secret letter to President Roosevelt warning of the nuclear threat.

Arthur Daley recalls a meeting with Moe in 1939. "He revealed what was in his heart. Moe said, 'Europe is in flames, withering in a fire set by Hitler. All over the Continent men and women and children are dying. Soon, we, too, will be involved. And what am I doing? Sitting in the bullpen telling stories to the relief pitchers.' "

During the 1940 and 1941 baseball seasons, while Moe was a coach with the Red Sox, he combined his scholarly pursuits with a greater interest in world political developments.

Berg rejected most offers to speak before organizations as the crisis worsened in Europe. He found time, however, to criticize fascism's book-burning rampage in a speech at a *Boston Herald* book fair at Boston Garden on October 24, 1940. He said, in part:

"As I looked about this book fair today, I thought of Paris, the Paris when it was still France, where a few years back, I first enjoyed browsing at the bookstalls along the Seine. These days will come back, they always do. History has a way of repeating itself — no wall or fortification determines the direction of real progress for long. More than two thousand years ago, the Emperor of China, Chin Shih-Huang, built the great wall to keep the enemy out, but the enemy came in. He was also the tyrant who burned all the Confucian books. Yes, they were burning books then, too; and not satisfied with burning the books, buried hundreds of scholars. I stood on that wall and saw the futility of it, but you all know that though the books of Confucius were burned, the spirit of Confucius still lives. I have looked out from the top of the pyramids, I looked out upon the conquest of Napoleon; they all fade away before the chance discovery of the enlightening Rosetta Stone found nearby in a small delta of the Nile. I have flown over the Maginot Line, since crumbled, but the spirit of Voltaire lives. All of which reminds me of Victor Hugo's arch-deacon of Notre Dame, whose mark you will remember. Architecture, seemingly so solid and durable, will yield to a little book made of paper. The book will destroy the building; spirit, ideas triumph over force. There are wall builders and book burners still rampant today, but they cannot win over our great wall, the wall of ideas as crystallized in the books you see around you tonight.

"And so all those walls and fortifications are but fleeting; only thought within the covers of a book is indestructible. I am optimistic enough to foresee a time when combat will be limited to those athletic outlets that give us a chance to let off steam innocently, to be fanatical about a Maribel Vinson on the ice, a Jack Dempsey in the ring, or the Red Sox. All of which represents democracy and heaven too. To drink from a fount of original essays, Montaigne said a few hundred years ago about Paris, is what I feel strongly about our way of life, our country: I love her so tenderly that even her spots, her blemishes, are dear unto me."

Moe's constant forays to Washington during the season ignited endless curiosity among his fellow ballplayers. Red Sox pitcher Elden Auker, one of the most expert submarine-ball hurlers in the American League, recalls: "We ballplayers felt Moe had some kind of relationship with the government, but we didn't know what it was. And Moe was basically a very mysterious man away from the ball park, so that added to the intrigue.

"We knew Moe well enough to realize it would be fruitless to ask him about it. You just didn't do that with Moe Berg. I did know, through Washington political friends, that he had some kind of relationship with Cordell Hull. Moe had a very keen grasp of what was going on in the world and as the picture in Europe got grimmer many of us ballplayers would ask Moe what he thought of the world situation. Moe believed war was unavoidable. I particularly remember one thing that he said which I found very interesting. It was either in the bullpen or on a train. It dealt with the concern over whether Mussolini would side with Hitler. So many of the top people in the country were concerned that, if Italy joined Hitler, it would mean double trouble. Well, Moe had an acute military mind. He reasoned that the best thing that could happen to the Allies would be for Hitler and Mussolini to join forces.

"This, of course, was contrary to the military thinking of the time. He theorized that, if Italy remained neutral, it would give the Allies no southern entrance to Germany and the Allies already were blocked from the east, west and north.

"If the unlikely happened and Italy joined the Allies, Hitler would overrun Italy and the German boundaries would be more expansive and so would German military strength in the country. By Italy joining Hitler, Moe felt the military advantage would be on our side."

As Germany's military might grew, there were several ballplayers and friends of Berg's who believed the catcher was involved in major espionage work. Pitcher Robert "Lefty" Grove, whose three hundred major league victories placed him in the Hall of Fame, spoke for them: "Some of the fellows thought Moe was an undercover man for the government. He had mysterious meetings and we didn't know what he was doing. I thought it was none of our business."

There were sketchy reports of Berg being in Europe in the winter of 1940, later validated. The *New York Times* years later reported, "Before the United States entered the war Berg helped hunt down Germany's atomic secrets by posing as a businessman in Switzerland."

But Tom Yawkey states, "I had no evidence that Moe Berg was a spy while with the Red Sox. Why, it would be inconceivable. But it would surprise me, knowing what I know now, if he hadn't engaged in some form of espionage during his tenure with us. You'd think he would drop a hint to those close to him, but he never let on. He never said anything to anybody. But that was Moe. No man came more decent, more mysterious or more secretive."

Research indicates that Moe Berg had spied for the American government during his baseball-playing years.

The precise number of these missions — which he performed without compensation — is unknown, but their intensity varied from major assignments to limited surveillance activity. Once, while in Germany in 1933, Berg made his way to a point five miles from the French border, and, in the darkness, opened a barn door. Inside were German fighter airplanes. He reported this to both the American and French governments. There are indications that Berg independently conducted surveillance, and that the aircraft discovery represented one of these activities. Whether his frequent visits to embassies entailed intelligence gathering is uncertain, but it is apparent that the government took advantage of Berg's considerable facility with languages. An additional reason why the government chose the catcher is the inescapable thought that an athlete would be the last person suspected of involvement in espionage.

And Samuel Berg said, "I never had any indication that my brother was a spy while a ballplayer but I'm not surprised that he agreed to carry out these missions. Moe was from an era and background that held strong loyalties to the country. Our parents were fiercely loyal and proud of America. This trait was reflected in Moe, I feel, when the government made requests of him. I'm sure that he was flattered that the government asked him to serve."

Suggestive of his parents' love of country is a letter postscript Moe received during 1941 spring training from his father, who wrote, "Love from Ma. She is knitting a pillow cover with 'God Bless America.' I do not think America has a truer patriot than she is."

In the spring of 1941, Berg's last season in organized

baseball and his second year as coach, the *Atlantic Monthly*, prompted by a suggestion from Anne Ford, sister of John Kieran's wife Margaret, asked him to write an article that would provide greater insight into baseball. The September issue of the *Atlantic* carried Berg's "Pitchers and Catchers" — considered the most scholarly article ever written on baseball.

In part, it reads:

I

Baseball men agree with the philosopher that perfection — which means a pennant to them — is attainable only through a proper combination of opposites. A team equally strong in attack and in defense, well-proportioned as a unit, with, of course, those intangibles, morale, enthusiasm, and direction — that is the story of success in baseball. Good fielding and pitching, without hitting, or vice versa, is like Ben Franklin's half a pair of scissors — ineffectual. Lopsided pennant failures are strewn throughout the record books. Twenty-game winners or .400 hitters do not ensure victory. *Ne quid nimis.* . . .

Many times a pitcher without apparent stuff wins, whereas his opponent, with what seems to be a great assortment, is knocked out of the box in an early inning. The answer, I believe, lies in the bare statement, "Bat meets ball"; any other inference may lead us into the danger of overcomplication. The player himself takes his ability for granted and passes off his success or lack of it with "You do or you don't." Call it the law of averages.

Luck, as well as skill, decides a game. The pitcher tries to minimize the element of luck. Between the knees and shoulders of the hitter, over a plate just 17 inches wide, lies the

target of the pitcher, who throws from a rectangular rubber
slab on a mound 60 feet, 6 inches distant. . . .

Because of this enforced concentration of pitches, perhaps
the game's most interesting drama unfolds within the limited
space of the ball-and-strike zone. The pitcher toes the mound;
action comes with the motion, delivery, and split-second flight
of the ball to the catcher. With every move the pitcher is
trying to fool the hitter, using his stuff, his skill and wiles, his
tricks and cunning, all his art to win.

Well known to ball players is the two-o'clock hitter who
breaks down fences in batting practice. There is no pressure;
the practice pitcher throws ball after ball with the same motion, the same delivery and speed. . . . This is an interesting
phenomenon. The hitter, in practice, is adjusting himself to
clock-like regularity of speed, constant and consistent. He is
concentrating on his timing. He has to coördinate his vision
and his swing. This coördination the opposing pitcher wants
to upset from the moment he steps on the rubber and the game
begins. The very duration of the stance itself, the windup
and motion, and the form of delivery are all calculated to
break the hitter's equilibrium. Before winding up, the pitcher
may hesitate, outstaring the notoriously anxious hitter in order
to disturb him. Ted Lyons, of the Chicago White Sox, master
student of a hitter's habits, brings his arms over his head now
once, now twice, three or more times, his eyes intent on every
move of the hitter, slowing up or quickening the pace of his
windup and motion in varying degrees before he delivers the
pitch. . . .

II

The importance of the bat has been stressed to such an
extent that, since 1920, foreign substances have been barred to

the pitcher, and the spitball outlawed. The resin bag, the sole concession, is used on the hands only to counteract perspiration. The cover of the ball, in two sections, is sewed together with stitches, slightly raised, in one long seam; today's pitcher, after experimentation and experience, takes whatever advantage he can of its surface to make his various pitches more effective by gripping the ball across or along two rows of stitches, or along one row or on the smooth surface. The pitcher is always working with a shiny new ball. A game today will consume as many as eight dozen balls instead of the two roughed and battered ones which were the limit in 1884. . . .

To fool the hitter — there's the rub. With an assortment at his disposal, a pitcher tries to adapt the delivery, as well as the pitch, to the hitter's weakness. Pitchers may have distinct forms of delivery and work differently on a given hitter; a pitcher throws overhand, three-quarter overhand (which is about midway between overhand and side-arm), side-arm, or underhand. A crossfire is an emphasized side-arm pitch thrown against the forward foot as the body leans to the same side as the pitching arm at the time of the motion and delivery. Not the least important part of the delivery is the body follow-through to get more stuff on the pitch and to take pressure off the arm. Having determined the hitter's weakness, the pitcher can throw to spots — for example, "high neck in," low outside, or letter high. But he never forgets that, with all his equipment, he is trying to throw the hitter off his timing — probably the best way to fool him, to get him out. Without varying his motion, he throws a change-of-pace fast or curve ball, pulls the string on his fast ball, slows up, takes a little off or adds a little to his fast ball.

Just as there are speed kings, so there are hitters without an apparent weakness. They have unusual vision, power, and great ability to coördinate these in the highest degree. They are the ranking, top hitters who hit everything in the strike zone well — perhaps one type of pitch less well than another.

To these hitters the pitcher throws his best pitch and leaves the result to the law of averages. Joe DiMaggio straddles in a spread-eagle stance with his feet wide apart and bat already cocked. He advances his forward foot only a matter of inches, so that, with little stride, he doesn't move his head, keeping his eyes steadily on the ball. He concentrates on the pitch; his weight equally distributed on both feet, he has perfect wrist action and power to drive the ball for distance. Mel Ott, on the other hand, lifts the front foot high just as the pitcher delivers the ball; he is not caught off balance or out of position, because he sets the foot down only after he has seen what type of pitch is coming. . . .

Rogers Hornsby, one of the game's greatest right-hand hitters, invariably took his position in the far rear corner of the batter's box, stepped into the pitch, and hit to all fields equally well. Ty Cobb was always a step ahead of the pitcher. He must have been because he led the American League in hitting every year but one in the thirteen-year period 1907–1919. He outstudied the pitcher and took as many positions in the batter's box as he thought necessary to counteract the type of motion and pitch he was likely to get. He adapted his stance to the pitcher who was then on the mound; for Red Faber, whose spitball broke sharply down, Cobb stood in front of the plate; for a curve-ball left-hander, Ty took a stance behind the plate in order to hit the curve after it broke, because, as Ty said, he could see it break and get hold of it the better. . . . Babe Ruth, because of his tremendous, unequaled home-run power, and his ability to hit equally well all sorts of pitches with a liberal stride and a free swing, and consistently farther than any other player, had demonstrated that he had the greatest coördination and power of any hitter ever known. Ted Williams, of the Boston Red Sox, the only current .400 hitter in the game, completely loose and relaxed, has keen enough eyes never to offer at a bad pitch; he has good wrist and arm action, leverage, and power. Jimmy Foxx, next to Babe Ruth as a home-run hitter, steps into a ball, using his tremendous wrists and forearms for his powerful, long and line drives. These hitters do not lunge with the body; the front hip gives way for the swing, and the body follows through.

III

The game is carried back and forth between the pitcher and the hitter. The hitter notices what and where the pitchers are throwing. If the pitcher is getting him out consistently, for example, on a curve outside, the hitter changes his mode of attack. Adaptability is the hallmark of the big-league hitter. Joe Cronin, playing manager of the Red Sox, has changed in his brilliant career from a fast-ball, left-field pull hitter to a curve-ball and a right-field hitter, to and fro through the whole cycle and back again, according to where the pitchers are throwing. He has no apparent weakness, hits to all fields, and is one of the greatest "clutch" hitters in the game. *Plus ça change plus c'est la même chose.*

. . . Lefty Grove was a fast-ball pitcher, and the hitters knew it. The hitters looked for this pitch; Lefty did not try to fool them by throwing anything else. . . . In 1935, Lefty had recovered from his first serious sore arm of the year before. Wear and tear, and the grind of many seasons, had taken their toll. Now he had changed his tactics, and was pitching curves and fast balls, one or the other. His control was practically perfect. On a day in that year in Washington, Heinie Manush, a great hitter, was at bat with two men on the bases. The game was at stake; the count was three balls and two strikes. Heinie stood there, confident, looking for Lefty's fast ball. "Well," thought Heinie, "it might be a curve." Lefty was throwing the curve more and more now, but the chances with the count of three and two were that Lefty would throw his fast ball with every-

thing he had on it. Fast or curve — he couldn't throw anything else; he had nothing else to throw. Heinie broke his
back striking out on the next pitch, the first fork ball Grove
ever threw. For over a year, on the side lines, in the bullpen,
between pitching starts, Lefty had practiced and perfected this
pitch before he threw it, and he waited for a crucial spot to
use it. Lefty had realized his limitations. The hitters were
getting to his fast and curve balls more than they used to. He
wanted to add to his pitching equipment; he felt he had to.
Heinie Manush anticipated, looked for, guessed a fast ball,
possibly a curve, but Lefty fooled him with his new pitch, a
fork ball. . . .

At first, the superspeed of Grove obviated the necessity of
pitching brains. But, when his speed began to fade, Lefty
turned to his head. With his almost perfect control and the
addition of his fork ball, Lefty now fools the hitter with his
cunning. With Montaigne, we conceive of Socrates in place of
Alexander, of brain for brawn, wit for whip. And this brings
us to a fascinating part of the pitcher-hitter drama: Does a
hitter guess? Does a pitcher try to outguess him? When the
pitching process is no longer mechanical, how much of it is
psychological? . . .

IV

We know that the pitcher studies the strength and weakness
of every hitter and that the hitter notes every variety of pitch
in the pitcher's repertory; that the big-league hitter is re-
sourceful, and quick to meet every new circumstance. Does he
anticipate what the pitcher is going to throw? He can regulate
his next pitch arbitrarily by the very last-second flick of the
wrist. There is no set pattern for the order of pitches. Possible
combinations are so many that a formula of probability can-

not be established. . . . And no human being has the power of divination. . . .

The few extraordinary hitters whose exceptional vision and power to coordinate must be the basis for their talent can afford to be oblivious of anything but the flight of the ball. Hughie Duffy, who has the highest batting average in baseball history (he hit .438 in 1894), or Rogers Hornsby, another great right-hand hitter, may even deny that he did anything but hit what he saw. But variety usually makes a hitter think. When Ty Cobb changed his stance at the plate to hit the pitcher then facing him, he anticipated not only a certain type of motion but also the pitch that followed it. He studied past performance. Joe DiMaggio hit a home run to break Willie Keeler's consecutive-games hitting record of 44, standing since 1897, and has since carried the record to 56 games. In hitting the home run off Dick Newsome, Red Sox pitcher, who has been very successful this year because of a good assortment of pitches, Joe explains: "I hit a fast ball; I knew he would come to that and was waiting for it; he had pitched knucklers, curves, and sinkers." . . .

V

The catcher squatting behind the hitter undoubtedly has the coign of vantage in the ball park; all the action takes place before him. Nothing is outside his view except the balls-and-strikes umpire behind him — which is at times no hardship. The receiver has a good pair of hands, shifts his feel gracefully for inside or outside pitches, and bends his knees, not his back, in any easy, rhythmic motion, as he stretches his arms to catch the ball below his belt. The catcher has to be able to cock his arm from any position, throw fast and accurately to the bases, field bunts like an infielder, and catch foul flies like an outfielder. He must be adept at catching a ball from any angle, and almost simultaneously tagging a runner at home plate. The catcher is the Cerberus of baseball.

These physical qualifications are only a part of a catcher's equipment. He signals the pitcher what to throw, and this implies superior baseball brains on his part. But a pitcher can put a veto on a catcher's judgment by shaking him off and waiting for another sign. The game cannot go on until he pitches. Every fan has seen a pitcher do this — like the judge who kept shaking his head from time to time while counsel was arguing; the lawyer finally turned to the jury and said, "Gentlemen, you might imagine that the shaking of his head by His Honor implied a difference of opinion, but you will notice if you remain here long enough that when His Honor shakes his head there is nothing in it." (Judges, if you are reading, please consider this *obiter*.) One would believe that a no-hit, no-run game, the acme of perfection, the goal of a pitcher, would satisfy even the most exacting battery mate. Yet, at the beginning of the seventh inning of a game under those conditions, "Sarge" Connally, White Sox pitcher, said to his catcher, "Let's mix 'em up; why don't you call for my knuckler?" "Sarge" was probably bored with his own infallibility. He lost the no-hitter and the game on an error. . . .

VI

Pitchers and catchers are mutually helpful. It is encouraging to a pitcher when a catcher calls for the ball he wants to throw and corroborates his judgment. The pitcher very seldom shakes a catcher off, because they are thinking alike in a given situation. By working together they know each other's system. Pitchers help catchers as much as catchers do pitchers. One appreciative catcher gives due credit to spit-baller Red Faber, knuckle-baller Ted Lyons, and fast-baller Tommy Thomas, all of the Chicago White Sox, for teaching him, as he caught them, much about catching and working with pitchers. . . .

The catcher works in harmony with the pitcher and dovetails his own judgment with the pitcher's stuff. He finds out quickly the pitcher's best ball and calls for it in the spots where it would be most effective. . . .

Taking the physical as well as the psychological factors into consideration, the pitcher must at times give even the best hitter his best pitch under the circumstances. He pitches hard, lets the law of averages do its work, and never second-guesses himself. The pitcher throws a fast ball through the heart of the plate, and the hitter, surprised, may even take it. The obvious pitch may be the most strategic one.

The pitcher may throw overhand to take full advantage of the white shirts in the bleacher background. Breaking balls are more effective when thrown against the resistance of the wind. In the latter part of a day, when shadows are cast in a stadium ball park, the pitcher may change his tactics by throwing more fast balls than he did earlier in the game.

The players are not interested in the score, but merely in how many runs are necessary to tie and to win. They take nothing for granted in baseball. The idea is to win. The game's the thing.

Edward Weeks, who edited "Pitchers and Catchers" for the *Atlantic*, termed the piece "literate, beautifully expressive and instructive. It demonstrated how prolific a student of baseball Moe was. He was a great favorite of mine."

Anne Ford, whose idea the article was, says:

"I remember being at a game and Moe was warming up a pitcher. He would catch the ball, turn to me and discuss his progress with 'Pitchers and Catchers,' throw the ball back, look at the pitcher, look at me, and discuss it further.

"Moe would come to our home in Brookline. He was fond of my father and mother. He moved in and out of your life. He was like a character in a play. Knock, knock and he enters, and just as suddenly would disappear. Moe was such a mystery. He always said the right thing and exuded warmth. Yet the sophistication seemed to be a facade. There wasn't a tenseness about Moe, but a little sadness, I think."

Margaret Kieran recalls, "Moe was fascinated about a chair in the house; it was a museum piece, really. It was either French or Spanish design with inlaid mother of pearl and a needlepoint seat. He insisted that my mother will it to him. He would kid my mother. He would place one hand on her and then on the chair, and say, 'Mother Ford, for me, dear, the chair — only for Moe.' And when he appeared some years later he said, 'Do you still have the chair Mother Ford? Remember old Moe.' "

During the spring of 1941, a series of letters were exchanged between the Office of Coordinator of Inter-American Affairs (CIAA) and Moe Berg. The coordinator was Nelson A. Rockefeller, then thirty-two. On March 5, 1941, Carl B. Spaeth, assistant coordinator, sent a letter to Moe care of the Boston Red Sox at Sarasota, Florida. It read:

Dear Mr. Berg:
    In connection with our plans for a sports program involving all of the American republics several people have suggested that you would undoubtedly be able to render a very real service. Your active participation in American sports, taken with your broad cultural background, certainly would serve to substantiate these recommendations.

Boston Red Sox at spring training camp in Sarasota, Florida. Moe Berg is in the last row, second from left. Next to him is Jimmy Foxx. Red Sox owner Tom Yawkey is in the second row, middle, in a dark suit. Joe Cronin, Sox manager, is to Yawkey's immediate left. Ted Williams is in the fourth row, extreme right. Bobby Doerr, star second baseman, is in the next-to-last row, second from left.

I hope that it may be possible for you to get to Washington for a day or two in the near future even though I know that you are now engaged in the baseball training season. If you are not able to see me before the team comes north, perhaps you can arrange to see me at that time.

Berg replied to Spaeth on March 16, 1941:

Thank you for your kind letter of March 5 which awaited
me in Sarasota following a short trip to Tampa and Miami —
hence the delay in answering you.

It is flattering to know that several people have suggested
me in connection with your plans for a sports program. I have
followed the work of your office as reported in the press and
would be honored and delighted to be able to help in any
possible way. As for the Red Sox spring training schedule, the
club practices or plays in Sarasota or vicinity until we break
camp on Tuesday, March 25. I believe I can arrange a flight to
Washington for a day, before that date, if necessary. After
leaving for the north it may be inconvenient to arrange a
meeting before Friday, April 11, when the club is in Baltimore
enroute to Boston.

The meeting between Moe Berg, Spaeth, Nelson Rockefeller and aides took place on April 11 in Washington. It
was followed by a series of other spring meetings at which
John Kieran was present.

On July 1 Rockefeller sent the following letter to Moe
Berg:

Dear Moe:

We appreciated very much your coming to Washington last
week. All present profited greatly by your participation in the
discussion and I can't thank you enough for the time and
thought you have given to this phase of our work. Enclosed
you will find a summary statement of the meeting. I should
like to have any comments or suggestions you care to make
concerning this.

On September 22, Spaeth wrote to Berg in Boston:

Dear Moe:

I have been advised by Asa Bushnell that he has several matters that he hopes you will consider with him as soon as the season is over. I have in mind our last conversation and wish to assure you that both Nelson Rockefeller and I are particularly anxious to have you work with us on this program. The exact work and the manner of its announcement will, I am sure, be determined to your entire satisfaction.

I see by the morning papers that the Sox have clinched second place. Congratulations.

On December 7, 1941, Japan attacked Pearl Harbor. Moe was at home when he heard the radio announcement and subsequent message by President Roosevelt asking Congress for a declaration of war.

Samuel Berg recalls Moe being in a reflective mood over the tragic events. "He told me, 'I feel sorry for the Japanese, as well as the Italians and Germans, who see things as we do.' He talked about his dear friend, Takizo Matsumoto. He felt terrible for him. He told me, 'Takizo must be having a very difficult time today.' "

Two days after the attack, Moe's father, Bernard, now seventy-one, lay in semistupor at Presbyterian Hospital in Newark dying of cancer. He wore a small American flag on his hospital johnny. He was informed the nation was at war.

"Where are the boys?" he asked.

Told that they were at home, Bernard asked in anguish, "And what are they doing there?" He was unaware that Moe had already agreed to accept a goodwill ambassadorship to Latin America as part of the Rockefeller group.

On January 14, Moe Berg announced he was leaving

baseball. Bernard Berg died the same day. Newspapers across the nation reported on Berg's entry into government service, with extensive copy outlining his baseball years. Many papers carried a small box noting his father's death.

The *New York Times* reported, "Today, as he quit the game he loved, Berg suffered a blow in the death of his father, Bernard Berg of Newark, N.J. after a long illness. The elder Berg also was a master of foreign languages reading six fluently."

The *Times*'s January 15, 1942, column on Berg's baseball retirement and appointment to a sensitive government job, said, "Morris Berg is a living antithesis of the Ring Lardner 'dumb' ball player." It assessed Berg as "baseball's foremost man of letters and his reputation as a scholar is not confined to the diamond world . . . an inch over six feet and powerfully built, Berg has been one of the popular players of the game. He doesn't flaunt his knowledge and doesn't like to be classified as linguist or lawyer or a lover of classical music. Instead he likes being called a baseball player . . ."

Thomas Meany reported in *P.M.* that "Moe has been studying the inroads of Axis propaganda in Central and South American countries for at least two years to my knowledge. He knew that several previous goodwill ambassadors of ours had unwittingly furthered this propaganda by adopting a patronizing attitude toward the peoples south of the Rio Grande.

"It is ironic that the suave and polished Berg should have been the subject of baseball's most illiterate message: 'Good field, no hit.' But it was so. Moe was with Brooklyn

at Clearwater in the spring of 1924 and so was Miguel
Gonzales, a coach for the Cardinals. Mike Kelley of Minneapolis wanted to buy Berg and wired Gonzales for his
opinion, which resulted in Miguel's famous four-word
telegraphic message of the young shortstop.

"Berg is destined to do a great job for his country. When
the final victory of the United Nations is achieved I ven-
ture that Moe's contribution will outweigh that of any
other athlete."

The *Christian Science Monitor* commented:

"If Moe Berg has permanently severed his coaching with
the Red Sox, the baseball players and writers have lost one
of their best friends. A diplomat to the extreme, he probably had more influence on the younger men of the ball
club than anyone else, not excluding Manager Joe Cronin.

"Often when the Red Sox were in Detroit, Moe Berg
would take trips across the Canadian border to chat with
influential friends on the war situation. A former foreign
correspondent of the *Monitor*, while returning recently
from Washington, found Moe closeted with a person very
high in international affairs and suspected the professor
was on official business."

Jerry Nason, the executive sports editor of the *Boston
Globe*, paid tribute to the catcher by reporting a little-
known linguistic enterprise undertaken by Berg in 1937.

Berg was then attempting, at the request of a group of
Japanese college professors, to provide an "L" sound to the
Japanese language, historically poor in terms of phonetic
variety. Nason wrote on January 15, 1942, "In spoken Japanese there is no L sound thus no letter in the Japanese
ideograph between K and M. Example: When the Japanese were advertising the Olympic games, which they were

originally to have sponsored in 1940, they spelled it 'Orympic Games.'

"Berg was determined to bridge the gap and did. A student of linguistic roots and their kinships, he softened the Japanese R with a *nigorti*, similar to the German umlaut, and induced the L sound." Nason added that Berg was preparing a paper on the matter for Kieo University when the Japanese moved full force into China. Berg withheld forwarding his work. "It was such a scholarly effort and when you consider it was done by a baseball catcher it warranted comment," Nason said. "But for Moe, it was simply a matter-of-fact undertaking. He simply never ceased to amaze."

Harvard Professor Wagner, after viewing Berg's *nigorti* figure, commented, "What occurred to Berg was that the Japanese syllabory has five written symbols which contain the R sound. By adding a Japanese *nigorti* sign to the upper right corner of the symbols at a slight angle, the reader was alerted to induce the L sound instead of the traditional Ra, Ri, Ru, Re, and Ro sounds." Wagner added that the project was obviously intended for use in foreign word translations.

The Associated Press asked Moe to comment on his immediate thoughts concerning Latin American relations with the United States. In a January 17 article carrying a Newark dateline, the AP said: "Moe Berg, released Wednesday by the Boston Red Sox to join the staff of Nelson A. Rockefeller, Coordinator of Inter-American Affairs, said today the program for solidifying the good neighbor policies 'must go on forever.' "

Al Schacht was asked to comment on the appointment.

He said, "Knowing Berg's appetite, I predict a food crisis in Latin America within six months."

Hundreds of sportswriters penned remembrances of Berg. Several writers recalled a bus carrying Red Sox players to an exhibition game in Georgia. It was night, and the bus driver had lost his way in bush country. The bus made a rest stop. When Berg returned to the bus he said quietly, "Mr. Driver, you're heading west and we should be moving east toward Atlanta." The driver asked Moe how he determined this. "So say the stars, Mr. Driver, so say the stars."

5

Latin
America

BEFORE EMBARKING ON HIS GOODWILL TOUR of Latin America, Moe Berg delivered an extraordinary radio address to the people of Japan, urging them, in Japanese, to lay down their arms and overthrow their warlords.

The broadcast, transmitted by powerful shortwave radio to Japan on February 24, 1942, was arranged by General William "Wild Bill" Donovan, head of the Office of Strategic Services (OSS), the infant spy agency. Berg himself would soon be an eminent OSS agent and confidant of Donovan.

"I speak to you as a friend of the Japanese people," Berg said, "as one who has studied the origins of your language, your history, your civilization, your progress, your adaptability, your culture, and I have found much to admire.

"It may seem presumptuous of me to speak to you, the Japanese people, while we are at war with you, but may I recall that I was greeted by thousands of you on two other and happier occasions: in 1932 when I was invited to coach your university students baseball, and two years later as a member of an all-American team.

"Fortunately, my visits brought me in contact with your younger generation — with youths building their minds and bodies in colleges and on athletic fields.

"I had friends among your older generation, too; revered college professors.

"I am able to talk to you somewhat in your own language, because I studied it in order to know you better. I lived among you, and traveled with intimate Japanese friends, to see your historic sites and appreciate your cultural history.

"I have admired the exquisite delicacy of your art, the woodprints of Hokusai, Toyokuni and Hiroshige.

"I stood on the bridge, sacred to you, in Kyoto, where Ushiwakamaru fought his famous battles.

"I journeyed to and admired the temples of Nikko and the Falls of Kegon No Taki.

"I admired the pagoda of Kofukuji in Nara, and saw a beautiful sunrise in the inland sea on the way to the island of Kysuhu.

"And I visited the hot springs of Kinugawa and Beppu, Kamakura, for a view of the Great Buddha, your pottery factory at Nagoya, and the silk mills at Utsonomiya.

"You have your traditions. I enjoyed marching with you to your sacred Meiji Shrine on November the third, celebrated with you Niinamesai, the holiday of the first rice crop of the year. Just ten years ago I watched, with thousands of you, the return of your Emperor from military maneuvers on his way across the Nijubashi. And my head too was lowered in reverence.

"Even in those days, when an excess of nationalism

seized upon many of you, still there were innumerable delightful contacts possible. You loved us enough to copy our national game — baseball. We appreciated it when thousands of you gave our all-American baseball team a great reception in 1934, waving American flags.

"Our team will never forget the great receptions not only in Tokyo, your capital, but also at Toyama, Sendai, Hakodate, Kamagori, Shizuoka, the Koshien Stadium at Kobe and at Moji, cities on three of your islands.

"We thought of you, then, the people of Japan, in your inherent love for us, as the rulers of your nation.

"And we still recall, too, the time when Count Okuma, the son of the founder of Waseda University, entertained our team in his private garden.

"I ask you, what sound basis is there for enmity between two peoples who enjoy the same national sport?

"And I remember yet another example of our great friendship. The first place my best Japanese friend wanted to visit in the United States was Fairhaven, Massachusetts. Why? Well, he wanted to visit the Whitfield home to revive memories dear to his heart. In June 1841, when Japan was isolated, closed, and the law of the land was penalty of death to any Japanese who left the islands and returned, Captain William H. Whitfield, the master of the whaling vessel *John Howland*, found a Japanese boy, Manjiro Nakahama, shipwrecked on the rock islands in the China Sea — the boy begged the captain to take him to America.

"As the captain wrote in his logbook, '. . . I could not understand anything . . . except that he was hungry.' The American captain took Nakahama, the boy, back to Fairhaven, educated him in private schools, and brought him up as a member of his family, so that later Nakahama became a foremost representative in the Commodore Perry negotiations which brought the United States and Japan together. Then later Nakahama became a professor in the Imperial University of Tokyo. He is the personification of the kindly relations between the peoples of our two countries.

"When Viscount Ishii presented a sword to the town of Fairhaven on behalf of his son, Dr. Toichiro Nakahama, he said: 'There is a wider significance to this grateful act of Dr. Nakahama than the simple recognition of a personal kindness. It is typical of that rising wave of sympathy and good understanding which begins to roll across the Pacific Ocean and promises to flood both lands with sweet waters of fraternity and goodwill.'

"That you did your biggest business with us, depended on us for your great silk exports and had free access to every port in the world with your goods, is something you well know.

"But this war is no great surprise to me. Exactly ten years ago I could see that war was imminent unless you, the Japanese people, could rise up and break the power of the warlords. Manchuria had already been taken by a ruse, a trick. Yet, when I was flying over the waters from Fukeoka on your west coast to Korea in 1932, I remembered that it was you, the Japanese, who had gallantly defended your homes and dispersed here the great Mongol fleet of the would-be conqueror Kubla Khan, in 1274; but in 1932 the Lytton Commission had just declared Japan guilty of aggression, and the violator of sacred treaties.

"From interviews with some of the college presidents in 1932 I learned that Japan was about to solidify her conquests, by leaving the League of Nations. Your military

men's interest in our then Secretary of State Stimson indicated to me this belligerent attitude against America's
nonrecognition principle. Stimson was representative of
all Americans in his belief in the sacredness of treaties; he
was not an isolated example.

"Count Soyeshima, the head of your Olympic Committee, on his return from Berlin in 1936, told me emphatically that the Germans were not the right partner for you.

"A few days after the all-American team had left Japan
in 1934, with the cheers of banzai ringing in our ears,
Shoriki, the publisher of the *Yomiuri Shimbun* was
stabbed. Why? Because of his interest in our trip, our
friendship and things American.

"I know your glorious history, about your samurai, the
Cult of Bushido, your love of the Confucian classics. I was
impressed by your hospitality and customs — all these
things I still admire. But you betrayed your friends — you
made a sneak attack on Pearl Harbor while your Ambassadors Nomura and Kurusu were carrying out diplomatic
conversations with us; you have lost face and are commit-
ting national seppuku.

"We assumed you were civilized even in battle — we
thought we saw that when we taught you our national
game and watched you play it. We thought that you played
and would fight according to rules.

"But, you have outraged us and every other nation in
the world with the exception of two — two that are tainted
with blood, Germany and Italy. They welcome you as
friends.

"But your temporary victories will bring you only mis-
ery.

"You cannot win this war. We and the twenty other republics of America are unified — we are united.

"Your leaders have betrayed you. They have misinterpreted democratic freedom and debate for weakness. The Matsuokas, your Jingoist army and navy officers, and your Axis partners, Hitler and Mussolini, have misjudged us, have misled you.

"After the war, a nation will have to be watched to prove its right to be partners among the civilized. We were patient and took much abuse. We humbly made many concessions. We tried to remain friends.

"Believe me when I tell you that you cannot win this war. I am speaking to you as a friend of the Japanese people, and tell you to take the reins now. Your warlords are not telling you the truth.

"The people of the United States and the people of Japan can be friends as they were in the past.

"It is up to you!"

President Roosevelt called Moe the next day, offering his and the country's thanks for the address.

After the war, many of Berg's Japanese friends, including some whom he, Ted Lyons and Lefty O'Doul had instructed in baseball, confirmed that they had heard the speech and been deeply moved by it. Some of them wept while they listened to the shortwave broadcast, realizing it was a friend talking to them from his heart.

Within a year of Moe's speech, Japanese officials banned baseball, branding it a decadent American sport.

On August 13, nine days before Berg's sensitive mission to Latin America began, the *Washington Post* wrote that

he was "going to Latin America as an extraordinary goodwill ambassador. His diplomatic mission is almost without
parallel in the annals of diplomacy."

Besides seeking to improve the welfare of U.S. servicemen stationed in Latin America and relations between
them and their hosts, Berg engaged in secret, high-priority
assessments of political figures. He sought to formulate an
accurate picture of Latin sympathies through discussions
with prominent citizens in both South and Central America.

For many decades, relations between the United States
and Latin American governments had been strained. During the war, the stigma *"el imperialista yanqui"* was a constant threat to America's military presence in Latin countries. The United States government was determined to
protect its southern flank against Nazi aggression and re-
lied on her Latin neighbors to form a solid hemispheric
block.

The job was not easy. Nazi propaganda characterized the
United States as the enemy of Latin America. The Germans funneled money to owners of newspapers and radio
stations, who attempted to rekindle or further inflame
Latin prejudices against the United States through false
news reports. Although all Latin nations, except Argen-
tina, severed relations with the Axis powers several months
after the United States entered the war, true hemispheric
solidarity remained a chimera. Naziphiles continued to
exist, particularly in the strategic area of northeast Brazil,
which was the takeoff point for U.S. fighter-bombers in the
African campaign.

John S. Dickey, a special assistant to Rockefeller in

Latin America and later president of Dartmouth College (1945–1970), remembers the concern over Nazi infiltration in South America and his meetings with Berg.

"I was handling the 'blacklist' sector of the department, which involved intelligence of Nazi or Axis firms doing business in South America.

"I first met Moe during the early years of the war. He was in the office in a rather informal way. We saw each other from time to time and enjoyed each other's company.

"I remember going with him to see the Senators play one day. It was a revealing experience for me. Moe wanted to be around ballplayers yet he had a compulsion to be shy. He wanted to be near these fellows and yet he didn't want much made of it. Ballplayers would recognize him and say something like, 'For God's sake, Berg, what are you doing here?' Moe would raise his hand to his lips and say, 'Ssshhh.'

"I remember we once spent two or three hours in which Moe elaborated, in effect, lectured me, I think, on the origin of the French word *oui*. I could only be amazed by the immense amount of his erudition. I came away from that get-together feeling that it was not an effort to impress, but rather, a genuine thing, a love of language.

"In a subtle way, Moe wanted to know what the Germans were up to in Brazil and elsewhere in South America. He would ask if I knew of some Nazi in South America. He was exceedingly discreet in what he said. I would see him in Washington and the next thing I knew he was off on a mysterious assignment to South America. He would come back, and not say anything of what he was doing. Being in intelligence, I understood."

Army Medical Corps Major Samuel Berg takes his brother for a jeep ride. The photo was taken near Riverside, California, in July 1942, just before Dr. Berg left for Australia. Moe was with Nelson Rockefeller's Inter-American Affairs group at the time.

Major Samuel Berg, M.D., taken while Dr. Berg was in the Pacific Theater of Operations during World War II.

In his secret report on Brazil, Berg told Rockefeller of discussions he had had with a number of prominent figures, including one on January 20, 1943, with Arturo da Silva Bernardes, Brazilian president from 1922 to 1926.

"Sitting opposite me, living in Rio, not exiled like his successor, Washington Luis, or the 1937 candidate, Armando Salles de Oliveira, Bernardes is a man of some sixty years," Berg wrote. "He told how he had devoted his life to Brazil, rising through successive political stages from his native Minas Gerais until he was the president, duly elected, of his country. He said that the U.S. and England, democracies, were answering the anti-democratic taunts of Hitler by outproducing the Axis even with the handicap of time, etc., that democracy must win, that democracy was, if not the best form of government, the 'menos mau' — 'least bad,' that policing of the aggressor nations under some form of league of nations was imperative. He expressed the opinion that he had given up his life for Brazil in vain because democratic government, as he knew it, no longer existed here since Getulio [President Getulio Vargas] had been in power since 1930 . . . and Brazil cannot be called a democracy when a man assumes power for over twelve years without elections. He said that the country was in bad condition and I gathered that Sr. Bernardes keeps up his contact with what is going on officially through people that he had appointed in his regime and were still sympathetic to him.

"He feared uprisings, caused by economic conditions, in this country shortly. As for himself he had no personal fear, and when he mentioned that he had been thinking of writing something along the lines that he was now speaking about — democracy, government, people — I assured him that one of our great old, conservative publications, of great repute and influence among our thinking people, *The Atlantic Monthly*, would be glad to publish anything that he would submit, and I further assured him that there was no better way to tell the American people that real democrats existed in Brazil than for him, a constitutional ex-president, to write this article.

"As for the attitude of the United States Government, officially and through its agents in its relations with Brazil, he expressed the opinion that, bearing in mind and appreciating what international relations entailed in the way of official protocol, courtesies, etc., no excessive tenderness should be shown to Getulio and the regime, that a 'medida,' a golden mean, should be reached in our dealings.

"I asked the ex-president if anybody from our Government, officially or unofficially, had spoken to him or been in contact with him in the past twelve years, and his answer was in the negative. He seemed anxious to talk, and very pleased with the opportunity of expressing himself."

Berg also met with retired General João Candido Castro, Jr., "who had already been imprisoned for disagreeing with this regime." Moe said the general told him of a bulletin criticizing the U.S. government that was issued by the Brazilian chief of staff and "read to all officials of the Brazilian army." Berg mentioned that the substance of the bulletin was that the United States had failed to carry out promises of aid. The bulletin was destroyed on orders from the general ten days after its publication. "This bulletin," Berg wrote, "comes from the official war headquarters of a country allied with us in a war, criticizing us . . ."

On February 4, 1943, Berg visited Major Juracy Magalhães at his home in Recife. He described the major as being governor of Bahia and a great friend of Getulio Vargas "until the coup d'etat of 1937 when Juracy resigned as the Governor."

Berg wrote, "He [Juracy Magalhães] said that Brigadier General Eduardo Gomes and General Mascarenhas de Morais, who has just been re-assigned to Rio from here, are great friends of the United States, inferring that Generals Francisco Paulo Adido, Alcio Souto, Newton Cavalcanti of the State of Alagoas, formerly military chief of the southern state of Parana, now coming here as Chief of the Army in this region, are definitely not in sympathy with our country.

"Juracy repeated the dread story I had heard from others in this coterie that General Eduardo Gomes, who was scheduled to go on the American plane to Ascension Island in the South Atlantic as a guest of our General Walsh, had to cancel at the last moment, and that the plane, with a number of American soldiers, has never been heard from. At least two other attempts have been made on the life of General Gomes by attacks on planes that he was scheduled to fly on; one has recently been shot down off the coast of Recife under mysterious circumstances killing all the Brazilian aviators aloft. The implication is that some Brazilian authorities are after General Gomes.

"Juracy, after telling me in detail the story of his life to give me background, said that he had officially written a plan of strategy for a possible African participation of a Brazilian Army unit but that the Brazilian Chief of Staff — General Dutra — had put a red line through this plan with the notation that no Brazilian soldiers are going to

Africa. The major named the Governor of Pernambuco, a fascist, as well as the military governor of the Island of Fernando de Noronha but said that the new interventor of Para, although named by Vargas, was not in sympathy with the regime."

Berg also met with some members of the Mesquita family, former owners of the influential newspaper *Estado de São Paulo*, which the government forced them to sell "at a loss." Moe reported that some of the Mesquitas were "in exile" because of government pressures.

Berg's report to Rockefeller said that the Brazilians he had met were "a proud people, want no help, but merely an assurance that if they help themselves we would not actively be against them. They express the opinion and seem to honestly believe that Ambassador [Jefferson] Caffery and some of our officials show a positive animosity toward them. At no time did they express or show any feeling except fondness for the United States and our institutions and the war against the Axis, and what is convincing, wanted to do nothing to disturb the status quo now that Brazil is in the war.

"It seems to me that these people would be a great continuing source of information to us."

Arriving in Panama in late August, Berg, after making protocol calls on Ambassador Edwin Wilson and members of the Panama government, went to Aircraft Warning Station No. 50, located seven miles from Almirante in the jungle.

"The jungle hereabouts bristles with bushmasters and coral snakes, baboons, jaguars and wild cats, and in the midst of it, barracks for 42 men," he wrote. "The listening device is on a hill, 800 feet above the barracks; the men are detailed in three shifts."

Berg's report said the men of Aircraft Warning Station No. 50 had but "two mitts and a soft ball," and with the help of natives, were clearing an area to be used as a ball field. Moe promptly requisitioned more athletic equipment and additional musical instruments to complement the one trombone they possessed.

On August 31, Berg flew to the U.S. airbase at Talara, Peru.

"It does not rain here, except sabbatically," he said in his report to Rockefeller. "There is no vegetation whatsoever — an arid, coastal plain. . . . The men [about four hundred and fifty servicemen] cannot swim in the ocean because of the sharks; the Peruvians put crosses as mourning markers on the beach where sharks have killed natives . . . the men need a movie theatre badly; also baseballs; softballs, volley balls, basketballs, radio and Victrolas, a reading room and library. My suggestion for books on Peruvian archeology, geology, history, folklore and legend was kindly received. The colonel [Homer Ferguson, in charge of the base] said some of the men had already done some scouting in the countryside."

He also noted in his report to Rockefeller a pervasive language barrier, which severely limited social contacts, and offered advice on instituting language courses that would alleviate the problem: "A Peruvian officer is being assigned to this base [Talara] and, as at every post, I suggested Spanish classes for the officers and men."

The language differences discouraged dating between the visitors and native women. As a result, U.S. servicemen

gravitated to houses of prostitution, which yielded an in-
credibly high rate of venereal diseases, particularly syphilis.

Berg was disturbed by the problem and reported a conversation with Colonel F. Edgar Cheatle, commanding
officer of the U.S. airbase at Salinas, Ecuador:

"Salinas was known from confidential reports as the
venereal Utopia, and the colonel assured me that it had
remained so. The venereal rate is very high — the highest
the past month, and ninety per cent was syphilis.

"The colonel had tried everything, had put La Liber-
tad, a seaside resort, and Guayaquil, the biggest city on the
Gulf, out of bounds, but there was further ingress of new
girls.

"He was now considering calling the very town of Salinas 'off limits' and I humbly suggested that he do that
only as a last resort so as not to reflect on the hospitality of
the Ecuadorian people, as well as on the lack of restraint
on the part of our boys.

"The local medical authorities were very cooperative,
had tried to eliminate all diseased girls; he [Cheatle]
would effect, with them, closer supervision of our boys on
leave as the best prophylactic measure. He said that tack-
ling the problem was like 'playing the xylophone — you
beat one bar down and the other pops up.'

"There was a building program on the post which did
not include a day room for the enlisted men. . . . I suggested that the colonel immediately order, locally, lumber,
roofing, etc., and gave him a check for this material and he
promised a recreation room in ten days. Perhaps this will
help restrict, to home, the soldiers' extracurricular activities."

Some commanding officers had other ideas for eliminating venereal diseases. Berg wrote, "At the other extreme, and it is my duty to report it, most of the commanding officers would like to exterminate the venereal plague by segregating the girls in a limited area, a stockade, under army and navy supervision, subject to a regular and rigid examination. . . . They even tell of certain commanders of our forces who heretofore have done this without fear of incurring the criticism of official Washington, the Fierce Look of the Organized Church or public opinion."

What rankled Berg more than anything else was the lack of meaningful relationships between the visitors and natives. Many areas offered opportunities to bridge the gaps but these were rarely seized. In Belem, Berg reported, "The officers at the Army Air Base have a club, frequented at too rare intervals by Brazilian officers." He wrote further, "The place to stress our democracy and democratic principles, and to teach away non-constitutional dictatorships of any kind and degree — the bitter lesson must now be clear to all freedom-loving people that the slightest touch of dictatorship poisons our life — is in the school, the university.

"The young student is impressionable. Exchange of students and teachers is vital for first-hand information about us and our democratic way of life. The teacher, with convictions, will, himself, scrutinize the texts and his fellow-teachers. The question of non-intervention in other sovereign nations' affairs, internal meddling, will not arise. Our example will be strong enough.

"More understanding North Americans ought to mingle with the Latins, speak their language and stress democracy in their talk and actions. We must let the real democrats, in the generic sense of the term, know where we stand, selfishly because it is vital to us and, unselfishly, as a matter of good neighborliness."

Berg's report struck a responsive chord in Nelson Rockefeller. In a letter to Berg, Rockefeller said:

Dear Moe,

I went over your report last night with a great deal of interest, and am looking forward to talking with you about it in the next day or so. I want to take this opportunity to tell you how much I appreciate all you've done for this Office and for the Government. Your work in assisting the Army to orient more effectively their units in South America to the various local problems has contributed greatly to the inter-American programs. Only someone with your experience and knowledge of international as well as human problems could have handled this situation with such tact and effectiveness.

Congratulations and very best wishes.

Sincerely,
Nelson

6

OSS

MOE BERG'S LATIN AMERICAN MISSION and previous work for his country while a professional baseball player came under the close scrutiny of top government and military officials. Among those privy to Berg's contributions was General William Donovan, director of the Office of Strategic Services. An imaginative, dynamic man, Donovan was a World War I hero who had become an extremely successful lawyer.

President Roosevelt lured Donovan from his law practice to assess the threat of Nazism on the Continent. After taking a tour of European and Balkan countries for Roosevelt in 1939, Donovan recommended the creation of an American spy agency abroad ˜whose functions, partly, would be to combat Nazi propaganda and engage in counterintelligence on Hitler's "new world order."

Donovan's plan was foreign to America. The civilian general, however, convinced Roosevelt of its usefulness, and the President established the Office of Coordinator of

Information in 1941, placing Donovan at its helm. This agency yielded to OSS, which was created in June 1942.

The new spy organization was composed of civilian and military personnel. Its network was global. American agents fought side by side with French, Italian, and Belgian resistance groups, while others spread anti-Nazi propaganda in Latin America. Some agents lived in caves behind Japanese lines in China and others followed Nazi arms development from Scandinavian listening posts.

Donovan recruited brilliant individuals, many of them prominent in the fields of business, education and government. He sought Berg for secret missions soon after the catcher joined Rockefeller's group, but Moe was committed to his Latin American mission. Upon completion of it, on August 1, 1943, he joined the OSS. Unlike the wide publicity generated by his appointment as goodwill ambassador to Latin America, silence surrounded Berg's entry into the intelligence organization.

Michael Burke, an OSS agent during the war and later president of the New York Yankees and Madison Square Garden Corporation, summarized the qualities that attracted Donovan to Berg: "Moe was absolutely ideal for undercover work. Not by design; just by nature. One, because of his physical attributes. He could go anyplace without fear. He had stamina. Also, he had that gift for languages. In addition, he had an alert, quick mind that could adapt itself into any new or strange subject and make him comfortable quickly. He was immensely involved intellectually and active in international affairs through reading and travel. He had the capacity to be at home in Italy or France or London or Bucharest. He was

on familiar ground in all those places. He also possessed a
great capacity for being able to live comfortably alone, and
could do this for long periods of time. The life of an agent
sometimes is a lonely one and some people aren't suited for
that."

Berg's ability to remain tight-lipped over his confidential activities in Japan and Latin America also attracted
Donovan. In addition, the catcher and the general had
parallel backgrounds. Both had attended Columbia Law
School and were Wall Street lawyers. Both were sports
enthusiasts and former college athletes. Donovan had
played football while at Columbia.

Berg's induction into OSS was followed by extensive
training in weaponry. He spent endless hours on the firing
range, practicing with rifles and pistols. He became a
marksman, and on most of his future missions, he would
carry either an Italian or a French handgun. Berg also took
parachute training in preparation for assignments behind
enemy lines. And, he was instructed in the use of potassium cyanide to prevent disclosure of secrets if captured.
The poisonous substance would kill him instantly.

Moe retained his civilian status during the war. He
could have assumed a simulated officer's rank, as did most
agents. He could have worn a uniform or carried credentials identifying him as a military officer. He did neither.
By remaining a civilian he was able to move more easily in
foreign countries, where he sometimes posed as a native.
But his decision increased the danger of his missions, since
those not in the military who were captured as spies were
generally shot instantly.

Moe's first major mission involved assessing the political

and military situation in Yugoslavia, invaded by the Germans in 1941. Besides fighting the Germans, Yugoslavia was embroiled in a civil war. The country's teenage monarch, King Peter, had fled to England during the German invasion, and two armies of Yugoslav resistance fighters battled each other for national supremacy.

One army was headed by Colonel Draža Mihajlovic, a Serbian. Mihajlovic's forces were known as the Chetniks and were loyal to King Peter. The other group, called the Partisans, was led by Josip Broz. A Croatian who was known as Tito, he had received his military training in Russia, was a Communist, and opposed the monarchy.

President Roosevelt ordered Donovan to evaluate the crisis in Yugoslavia to determine which resistance army should get American aid. A number of secret missions were launched, beginning in the late summer of 1943 and continuing through the fall and winter.

Berg entered Yugoslavia on a solo mission in the fall of 1943. Bob Broeg, *St. Louis Post-Dispatch* sports editor, wrote that Berg may have entered the country by parachute. Arriving at the mountain headquarters of Mihajlovic, Moe conferred with the Serbian leader for several days. Berg next visited Tito's camp, spending about one week with the latter's aides.

Berg later informed Donovan that Tito forces were superior and had the backing of the people. His report corroborated earlier assessments by British and other American missions. Indeed, Churchill withdrew official support of Mihajlovic and recalled the British mission operating in his territory early in December 1943. The United States, however, never adopted a firm policy on Yugoslavia. Although Roosevelt agreed to support Tito at the Big Three Conference in Teheran, the United States continued dividing aid between the two warring factions. By the time America moved toward a solid pro-Tito position, it was too late. The Russians, with Tito's approval, marched into Yugoslavia, dooming American-Yugoslav rapprochement.

After Yugoslavia, General Donovan called upon Moe Berg to undertake further critical assignments.

"Moe became a great favorite of Donovan's," says Burke.

Otto Doering, Donovan's executive officer, adds, "I know Donovan thought very highly of Moe Berg. He thought him a courageous man and an extremely able agent."

However, Berg was not without at least one critic. After his selection for a sensitive assignment in Italy, a Donovan aide, unaware of Berg's credentials and closeness to the general, remarked, "Do you know who they gave us for this mission? A ballplayer named Moe Berg. You ever hear of him?"

"Yes," Donovan replied. "He's the slowest runner in the American League."

The race for the atomic bomb between Germany and the United States was the most consequential struggle in the progression of man.

Only a few individuals were aware of this life-and-death contest. Never in history was a rivalry of such proportions so effectively hidden from men at war and the home front. America's atomic bomb program, the Manhattan Project, was so secret that Vice-President Harry S. Truman was unaware of it. Truman was informed only after assuming the presidency upon the death of Roosevelt in April 1945.

But Moe Berg, the catcher, knew that America was racing against time for the ultimate weapon, and survival.

Secret U.S. government documents show that Berg was America's premier atomic spy during World War II and that he played a vital role in gathering information on the work of Germany's major scientists. Berg's involvement in the rush for the bomb stemmed from fear that Germany was ahead of the United States in its development.

General Leslie R. Groves, in charge of the Manhattan Project, placed the highest priority on a determination of where Hitler stood in building the awesome weapon. Groves's concern was heightened by key foreign scientists working on the Manhattan Project who held unwavering respect for German science.

Army Major Robert Furman, who escorted half of the first atomic bomb aboard the U.S.S. *Indianapolis* to Tinian Island on its way to Hiroshima, recalls: "This fear these foreign-born scientists had of German efforts was keeping them awake nights. They had a real appreciation of German science and were very nervous about Germany's atomic development. American scientists did not share this concern. Groves sent me to Chicago to meet with scientists there and in Oak Ridge, and Hanford, and Los Alamos. The purpose was to see what could be done about alleviating their fear."

The meetings between Furman and the scientists resulted in General Groves taking command of all atomic counterintelligence. Until Groves's action, the various intelligence agencies — OSS, army G-2, navy ONI, and lesser units — had been operating independently of one another in atomic spying. None of the spies at that time knew about the race for the bomb. Atomic espionage was only a part of their overall activities. Often information Groves needed was delayed or lost in a bureaucratic shuffle.

Commenting in his book *Now It Can Be Told*, Groves said, "In the fall of 1943, General Marshall [George C. Marshall] asked me, through Styer [Major General W. D. Styer] whether there was any reason why I could not take over all foreign intelligence in our area of interest. Apparently, he felt that the existing agencies were not well coordinated; and that, as a result, there were many gaps not being covered. Moreover, it was probable, he thought, that these agencies would not always recognize the particular importance to us of some of the information they might receive, since, for security reasons, we had to limit the number of outsiders to whom we needed to explain the kind of information we wanted."

With extreme care and deliberation, the selection of atomic spies from army and navy intelligence and OSS began. Only the most trustworthy, intelligent and courageous individuals were considered.

General Groves visited General Donovan, seeking this rare composite from OSS. According to William Casey, chief of OSS Secret Intelligence in Europe and now chairman of the Export-Import Bank of the United States, "Donovan gave him Moe."

Groves weighed Berg's selection as a fully informed atomic spy against the obvious drawback — Moe's exposure. As the nation's most intellectual athlete, much had been written about Berg in countries throughout the world. Magazines and newspapers in Axis nations had reported on his baseball play and brightness. His picture often accompanied the stories. An inherent danger would persist in Berg's carrying out some of the most sensitive missions of the war. The ideal, militarily and strategically, would be the selection of an unknown. Groves concluded, however, that Moe's assets, including past missions, far outbalanced the one drawback.

One of these missions involved the heavy water plant in Rjukan, Norway. The Germans had banked their hopes on building an atomic bomb on heavy water. The rare fluid acts as a moderator to control fissioning uranium atoms so that they can be used as a source of energy. The only place where heavy water was being produced in quantities was at the Rjukan plant. The Germans had occupied Norway since 1940 and forced the operators of the plant to produce heavy water for them for shipment to laboratories in Berlin.

Acts of sabotage were committed on the plant to hamper production. The most successful one occurred in February 1943, when, in a daring raid by Norwegian saboteurs, the plant was virtually destroyed. First reports indicated that the attack would cripple heavy water production for two years. But by the spring of 1943, word leaked out of Scandinavia that the Rjukan plant had resumed part of its operations. Intelligence gathering on the plant continued through the summer and fall. In mid-October, Berg was picked to enter Norway and determine the plant's status. He flew from England in a U.S. military plane that dropped him into Norway. He was met by Norwegian resistance fighters who assisted him in traveling to Oslo.

Berg questioned scientists in Oslo concerning activity at the Rjukan plant, located some seventy-five miles away. They told him monthly heavy water quotas were more than half the level before the February attack. Berg left Norway on an American military plane, which had landed in a remote area to take him back to England.

In a meeting with Donovan, Berg provided the OSS director with his detailed report on the Norwegian heavy water plant. This information was relayed to Groves. More intelligence reports followed Berg's mission, hardening the military view that the plant must be destroyed.

An air attack was ordered, ending Germany's production of heavy water in Norway. German officials theorized that further use of the plant would encourage more bombing, and ordered all salvageable plant equipment shipped to Germany, where heavy water research installations were under construction.

Another early Berg mission occurred in Naples. He hoped to establish what the degree of German, and possibly Italian, atomic development was from Naples scientists, but failed to learn anything. The scientists reaffirmed what Groves, Donovan and Berg believed: that the foremost brains in Italian science lay in German-occupied Rome.

One day, while Moe was in Naples, he was standing on a street corner when a trio of Americans walked by. They were Vernon "Lefty" Gomez, Jack Sharkey, the former heavyweight boxing champion, and Fred Cochrane, business manager for several athletes.

They immediately recognized Moe.

"Wherever I go in this world I bump into Moe Berg,"

Gomez says in recalling the first thought that crossed his mind. "I went over to him and said, 'Hello, Moe,' as did the others. Moe responded by putting his finger to his lip and whispering 'Ssshhh.' He looked mysterious and kept looking around. Moe apparently did not want to talk. I got a little upset by this and we just kept on going toward the front, where we were to entertain the troops. Humphrey Bogart and Joe E. Brown were ahead of us. The entire incident lasted just seconds."

Cochrane recalls, "Well, I was put out as much as Lefty. After all, I had been very close to Moe during his Red Sox days. We walked away from him unable to understand how we were going to hurt him by talking to us. But you had to admire him. Moe was living a command performance and lived up to its dictates. It was symbolic of the man's whole life, one which was threaded with secrecy."

Originally, General Donovan selected Berg for scientific assignments because of the catcher's linguistic skills. Moe did not have a high aptitude in science in high school or college.

"Moe was awful in science in school," recalls Dr. Berg. The grasp of the fundamentals of the highly specialized field of atomic physics and their practical applications did not require extraordinary effort, however. In the assessment of Dr. Henry D. Smyth, eminent Princeton physicist, "Moe Berg had a brilliant mind and I think could have picked up the information he needed in his missions in two to three weeks of study."

Moe's studies included reading how the German chemist, Dr. Otto Hahn, split the uranium atom during an experiment and that it was Dr. Lise Meitner, a former long-time colleague of Hahn's, who explained what he had achieved. That information was available in popular magazine articles published before the United States entered the war.

Further, his studies revealed that before an atomic bomb could be made, the rare isotope U-235 has to be separated from the more abundant U-238 and purified. He learned that one pound of pure U-235 has the explosive power of fifteen thousand tons of TNT and that if a mass of one pound of U-235 could be converted into energy it would yield the equivalent of 5,875,000,000 pounds of coal. In addition, he learned where uranium was mined and how much thorium, which is also fissionable, was available on the European continent. He learned of the importance of heavy water in experimentation and acquired knowledge of basic scientific terminology — neutrons, protons, nucleus, cyclotron — and their functions. Also, to operate effectively as an atomic undercover agent, he learned the names of the important atomic scientists, their specialties and discoveries.

Again, much of this material was available in scientific journals and library primers, but to widen his overall understanding, Berg took the personal approach: he associated with some of the world's leading scientists and literally picked their brains.

One of Moe's closest friends was Dr. Howard Percy Robertson, distinguished mathematical physicist who had served on the faculty of Princeton University for eighteen years and later, before his death in 1961 from injuries suffered in a car accident, was scientific adviser to President John F. Kennedy.

According to Dr. William Fowler, professor of physics at California Institute of Technology, Dr. Robertson "had exceptional mathematical powers coupled with a deep insight into physical processes. Early in his career he gave the solution of Einstein's cosmological equations for the case of a homogeneous and isotropic universe. This solution is incorporated in the 'line element' which bears his name."

During the war, Dr. Robertson was scientific liaison officer for the Office of Scientific Research and Development in London. His son, Dr. Duncan Robertson, a Tucson, Arizona, surgeon, relates, "Moe met my father in London during the war and they became very good friends." The great scientific mind of Dr. Robertson lay open to Berg. With Robertson serving as Berg's personal mentor, the pair would escape to the English countryside, where Moe became a one-man student body of the famous physicist.

Berg's knowledge had now advanced to the stage of determining whether Germany or Japan was capable of building an atomic bomb. He had learned that three basic ingredients were needed to build a bomb: qualified scientists, industrial might, and uranium or thorium.

Germany was rich in the first two areas, but it was questionable whether it had enough uranium and highly doubtful that there was an adequate supply of thorium, (principally produced in Brazil) available on the Continent. Japan was deficient in all three areas.

One of Berg's early OSS reports, filed in January 1944, disclosed that a shipment of nearly seven hundred tons of Belgian Congo uranium ore had been delivered to Duisburg, Germany. This development, coupled with similar reports that uranium ore from mines in Joachimsthal, Czechoslovakia, were being shipped to Berlin, indicated

Germany had the basic fuel to build an atomic bomb.

Orders were given to bomb Duisburg and nearby areas, to avert suspicion of the real purpose for the raid. The bomber pilots and crews were not briefed on the precise reason for the attack. This strategy was always employed in sensitive bombing raids in the event a plane was shot down and its crew interrogated.

Duisburg was devastated by wave after wave of American planes, which dropped bomb tonnage equaled only at industrial Dusseldorf and Leipzig.

Moe received several assignments from Lieutenant Colonel H. K. Calvert, head of the Manhattan Project's liaison office in London. As Groves's European representative, Calvert had extraordinary power. He operated under a cover name and was given three desks, one at the headquarters of European Theater of Operations, U.S.A., another at the American Embassy, where his title was Assistant Military Attaché, and a third at the British Atomic Energy Office, whose code name was Tube Alloys.

Thousands of pieces of intelligence from a worldwide network were funneled to Calvert, including those from underground organizations, former POWs and refugees. Calvert daily read all raw intelligence information dealing with enemy scientific work and arms development.

"Ninety-nine percent of the material we received was ungraded," the peacetime oilman-lawyer from Oklahoma recalls. "By ungraded, I mean they may not carry a date or a location. They were of unknown reliability. The information we received was only as good as its source. That's where Moe entered the picture.

"As far as I know, Moe did not have an office in London. He would appear suddenly out of the blue and then disappear just as mysteriously. He was a loner and was always on the move. I would see him with his pockets stuffed with pieces of paper that he had scribbled notes on.

"Moe was the only agent we used from our London office to visit and interrogate the sources circling Germany. He was out to get all the information he could by picking the brains of every scientist, mainly in the atomic area."

Pinpointing the work and locations of Hitler's top scientists was Berg's main priority. In Calvert's words, "We built dossiers on all the top German atomic scientists. There were numerous others — the younger ones — working on atomic development that we had no information on. Our strategy was to go after the top ones, who could lead us to the others."

The list of German scientists included Professor Werner Heisenberg, Nobel Prize winner, who, intelligence reports indicated, was in charge of a group working on separating U-235 from U-238; Professor Max von Laue, Nobel Prize winner in 1914; Professor Walther Gerlach, head of the atomic energy project; Dr. Kurt Diebner, leader of a group working on an uranium reactor; Professor Paul Harteck, specialist in separating uranium isotopes and in the production of heavy water; Dr. Erich Bagge, who also specialized in isotope separation; Dr. Karl Wirtz, a leading physicist connected with Heisenberg's group; Dr. Horst Korsching, a member of a second team working on separating U-235 from U-238; Professor Carl Friedrich von Weizsäcker, brilliant young physicist; and the esteemed Dr. Otto Hahn, splitter of the atom.

These scientists were believed to be building an atomic bomb for Hitler. But their whereabouts was a mystery. Many of them had been in Berlin, but from August 1943, through the following winter, the German city had been heavily pounded by Allied raids, forcing most scientists to evacuate.

Berg's role in finding them, according to Calvert, "lay in going to neutral countries initially. We had had no contact with scientists in neutral countries."

In the spring of 1944, Berg entered Switzerland to establish ties with pro-Allied scientists. His objective was to cultivate Swiss scientists and learn what they knew about the German atomic threat and where the important enemy scientists were living. The Swiss scientists were in a favorable position to know these things since German scientists often crossed into Switzerland during the war to lecture or confer with colleagues. Most of this activity was carried on in Zurich.

Moe soon struck gold. Through a Swiss contact he learned that Heisenberg was living near Hechingen in the Black Forest region. The contact — Professor Paul Scherrer, an outstanding experimental physicist — had ascertained Heisenberg's address after he received a letter from him with the Hechingen postmark.

Additional evidence coming from a reliable British source inside Germany disclosed other German atomic scientists had been seen in Hechingen. Further intelligence reports indicated many of Germany's secret scientific projects had been moved from bomb-ravaged Berlin to Bisingen, situated three miles south of Hechingen.

Put together, these bits of information began to pinpoint Hechingen-Bisingen as Germany's atomic bomb center. American aerial photo reconnaissance teams zoomed in over the area, taking pictures that were enlarged, studied, and which showed slave labor camps in Bisingen. Manhattan Project officials at first believed this was the beginning of the enemy's "Oak Ridge."

Pressure to bomb Bisingen intensified but, in his memoirs, General Groves stated he was against immediately bombing the area, fearing the Germans would move deeper underground. And, as it turned out, British mining experts studying pictures of the Bisingen site determined that the facility was a shale oil–cracking plant.

Manhattan Project officials remained uncertain over exactly what was going on in the fairylike villages of the Black Forest. They wrestled with the idea of sending someone into Hechingen-Bisingen to determine what Hitler's top atomic scientists were doing.

Calvert learned of a clergyman in London who had been vicar of Bisingen and was thoroughly familiar with the area. The vicar was contacted by Calvert and shown the aerial photos of Bisingen. He pointed out and identified landmarks for Calvert.

After painstaking consideration, Calvert decided to send Berg into Bisingen. He held a meeting with him and the pair discussed the matter. The mission was extremely dangerous but Calvert said, "Moe was an intense man and would do anything to get the job done."

For days, Berg studied the dialect of the region he was to penetrate. As was his espionage modus operandi, he also studied the area's historical past and present, and its prominent local figures. Before he was to leave, Moe was given specially tailored clothing that matched the styles worn in Bisingen.

"I saw Moe the night before he left," William Casey, OSS secret intelligence chief in Europe recalls. "We were sitting around the Hotel Claredge in London and he told me all these stories about Babe Ruth and Ted Lyons. He took off to Switzerland the next day. He said he was going to try to find Heisenberg."

But the planned entry into Germany never materialized. General Groves canceled it. In his memoirs, Groves recalled, "When I heard of Calvert's plan for Berg to go into the Hechingen-Bisingen area, I immediately stopped it, realizing that if he were captured, the Nazis might be able to extract far more information about our project than we could ever hope to obtain if he were successful."

Calvert adds, "Looking back on it, Groves was correct. Moe knew more than you would want him to know. I doubt if he knew where our installations were located. But, if he were caught, it would not have taken much for the Germans to add a few things together and alert them of our atomic efforts." Further, the possibility remained that Moe would not have the chance to swallow cyanide.

Moe often returned to London following his assignments. He loved the city and spent many leisure hours in museums or libraries. His social life was low-key. "He didn't like to go into the big places too often," Calvert said. "He was more for the quiet dining room."

There was one special woman in Moe's life in London, a Scandinavian, according to OSS agent Michael Burke: "I introduced her to Moe. Then I was off parachuting into

France and she and Moe became great friends. We talked about her later. He was very fond of her."

Burke and another OSS man, Henry Ringling North, of the famous circus family, took a flat in the West End on Limehouse Docks, where Moe used to visit them.

"Moe was an inexhaustible walker," Burke remembers. "On Sundays he used to come to our flat and we'd have breakfast. Then we'd start walking about London. He'd walk our legs off. He'd walk fifteen or twenty miles. He had an enormous familiarity with a lot of places in London and elsewhere in Europe.

"I remember once going to an old bookshop on a place called Meard Street. He said he wanted to show us this great shop and so we hiked four miles to get to it. We went through the front door and up a flight of rickety stairs. It was very dimly lit on the second floor and Moe made his way with great familiarity down along the book stacks. He picked one off the shelf — meantime, he had reached up and found a naked light bulb and turned it on, one he'd turned on maybe a hundred times before — opened the book and said, 'Isn't this wonderful. I studied under him at the Sorbonne.'

"Imagine. We had walked four miles for this. Moe did get an enormous sense of satisfaction and delight out of little things like that; knowing that the book was still there from a few years before."

"I think," Burke continues, "what brought us together was our sports background. I knew him as an ex–big leaguer and he had heard of my playing football at the University of Pennsylvania. There were a number of peo- ple around England that used to think Moe and I were brothers. Couple of people used to say to me, 'Your brother Moe did this or that.' We used to kid each other about it and take turns introducing ourselves as the Berg Brothers or the Burke Brothers."

North used to tease Moe about always wearing dark clothing. "One day," Burke recounts, "Henry was in Paris and went to a haberdashery and bought Moe a tie. When he presented it to Moe, Henry said, 'Moe, this is an extravagant tie. You'll be dazzled by its bright colors.' Moe opened the box to find a black tie with a black design embossed on it."

Generals Groves and Donovan, seeking to allay any miscalculation, ordered Moe to Rome in June of 1944 to determine whether Italian scientists were working on an atomic bomb. His mission also included the interrogation of these scientists about their knowledge of Germany's atomic profile.

Elaborate plans were drawn to deliver Berg into Italy. A secret government document said a submarine would be dispatched to pick up Moe somewhere on the east coast of Britain. From there, it was to proceed to the Mediterranean, where it would deposit the catcher on the Italian west coast, south of Rome. A military unit was scheduled to await him there.

Italy's foremost atomists lived in Rome, which was under German occupation at the time. Groves did not want these scientists, particularly those sympathetic to the Allies, to buttress Germany's scientific corps in what was to be the last year of the war. Several Italian scientists had already been taken to Germany and Berg's directive was to smuggle those remaining safely out of Italy.

Implementation of the submarine plan, however, was halted hours before its execution when regrouped Allied forces battled through weakened defenses at Anzio and the Gustav Line and liberated Rome. Consequently, Moe was flown to the Eternal City on June 6, 1944, the day Normandy was invaded.

The Wehrmacht was now being attacked on all fronts. But Hitler continued to voice confidence that his scientists were on the verge of delivering *Wunder Waffen* — wonder weapons — which would reverse the course of the war and lead to German world conquest.

Berg was met in Rome by Andrew J. Torrielli, an intelligence officer, who is now a professor of languages at Loyola University: "We had been informed that Berg was sent over on the direct orders of General Donovan. As I recall, the day I met Moe was the hottest in memory. I went to the public square in Rome and there he was, dressed in a blue serge suit and carrying a large suitcase."

Moe had been briefed on his mission by Dr. Robertson in London. A secret government document written by Lieutenant Colonel Howard W. Dix, in charge of all atomic counterintelligence collected by OSS, said Moe's primary targets were Dr. Eduardo Amaldi and Dr. Gian Carlo Wick, professors at the University of Rome before the German occupation.

Wick was a theoretical physicist, while Amaldi was Italy's top atomic scientist. Both scientists had been associated with Enrico Fermi, Nobel Prize–winning physicist who, with his family, fled Mussolini's fascist state for the United States in 1939.

Laura Fermi, wife of the famous physicist, recalls the association between her husband, Wick and Amaldi:

"Wick came as a young assistant to my husband at the University of Rome where he finished his training.

"Amaldi and my husband worked on many projects together. Their main work was the study of the properties of neutrons and the radioactivity produced by neutron bombardment. This study was conducted between 1934 and 1938."

In America, Fermi continued his exploration of the mysteries of the atom, and under his leadership the controlled release of atomic energy was achieved for the first time during a self-sustaining chain reaction of a uranium atom on December 2, 1942. This was recorded underneath the grandstand at Stagg field at the University of Chicago. The feat was a milestone in man's efforts to exploit the enormous energy of the uranium atom.

Berg found Wick and Amaldi shortly after arriving in Italy. "I met Moe just after the Allies had come into Rome," Dr. Wick, who now teaches at Columbia University, relates. "I had been in hiding. Moe invited me to dinner on a couple of occasions. He asked all types of questions concerning our atomic projects and the German work in this area. The fact is, we were not working on an atomic bomb or atomic weapons. Also, we knew virtually nothing about the German efforts.

"Moe asked me if I knew the whereabouts of the important German scientists. I did not have any information about that either."

Dr. Amaldi, who still teaches at the University of Rome, describes Berg going to his home and questioning him "about what was going on in Italy in the field of the application of nuclear physics.

"I explained that nothing was going on in Italy because
the physicists who had the capacity to operate in this field
had decided, at the beginning of the war, to stay away from
any activity which might be connected with atomic applications — in particular those connected with war.

"Berg asked me what I knew about German research in
this field, but, unfortunately, I had no information at all.
He asked me to go to Naples the same day, where he would
arrange to bring me to the United States, but I refused to
leave since I did not see any use or scope in such a trip.
The conversation went on for some time on this point and
finally Berg stopped insisting on my trip.

"In the successive days, Berg visited us a few times more
and also on these occasions the conversation was of the
same type as the first day, but I was not able to add more
information or to change my mind about a trip to America."

Berg's report to OSS headquarters in Washington concluded that Italy posed no atomic threat. He also expressed
confidence that Italian scientists knew nothing about
German atomic development. His report was sent directly
to General Groves by Colonel Dix.

Unable to cut through the shroud surrounding Germany's atomic bomb project, Berg remained in Italy to
investigate scientific activities in other fields. Armed with
profiles on leading figures in the areas of aeronautics, rocketry, jet propulsion, and biological and chemical warfare,
Moe rented an apartment near the Villa Borghese in
Rome.

After scouring the dossiers on the scientists, Berg decided Professor Luigi Crocco, a jet propulsion expert, was

one of the most important. Crocco was allowed to live and work in Rome during the German occupation but, in his words, "had a hiding place all picked out at the University of Rome. I didn't have to use it, because the Americans entered Rome and the Germans left."

"Moe came to see me twice. He was very sympathetic and, also, very serious. He asked me for information about my activities. I told him about my work and research in jet and rocket engines, a field the English and Germans felt was very critical. Moe asked me about Germany's efforts but we didn't know really what was going on."

American and British intelligence had placed importance on a theoretical physicist living near Pisa. He had adamantly rejected an Allied appeal to discuss atomic developments. Intrigued by the scientist's reputation for being a Petrarchan scholar, Berg made arrangements to confer with him. Moe entered the scientist's home in the cover of darkness.

The elderly physicist shook hands with the catcher, then emphasized he would not discuss military or scientific matters.

Moe walked toward the scientist's bookshelf and removed a volume of Petrarch. He handed it to his host.

"I think your friend Petrarch would discuss them fully," Berg reportedly commented. He looked at the scientist and, then, quoting in Latin from Petrarch's "Italia Mia," said:

> *Is this not the dear soil for which I pined?*
> *Is not this my own nest*
> *Where I was nourished and given life?*

Is not this the dear land in which we trust,
Mother loving and kind
Who shelters parents, brother, sister, wife?

The scientist was obviously jolted by Berg's recital of
Petrarch's canzone of national honor. The suggestion that
Petrarch, himself, was speaking in condemning and pleading verse to the reticent physicist appeared effective. The
two men discussed Petrarch for three days, each lunging
into Petrarchan verse. They concurred that Petrarch's
mysterious love "Laura" had lived and critics' contentions
that she was an imaginary love undeserved. Laura alle-
gories, in the original Italian, came to life.

Once in the greenwood hunting, all alone.
I came upon my wild one, fierce and fair,
in a pool bathing, bare,
while the hot sun incontinently shone.
And since no other sight could so delight me,
I greedily stared, and she was anger-shamed;
and in my eyes — a vengeful reprimand —
she splattered water with the heel of her hand.

They toasted Petrarch with wine and both agreed no
human in the history of civilization had ever represented
humanism as he did. Recital of the stirring verses by Italy's
greatest poet ultimately yielded to discussion of atomic possibilities. It is impossible to determine precisely what Berg
learned, but research indicates the physicist expressed confidence that atomic weapons, in some form, would be perfected by Germany. There was also discussion of an Italian

admiral named Eugenio Minisini, an authority on torpe-
does.

During Moe's research the name Antonio Ferri surfaced
constantly. Moe had studied the file on Ferri, but it contained nothing exceptional. It assessed Ferri simply as an
aeronautical engineer who had abandoned his career in
1943 to join a partisan group.

But additional probing into Ferri's background established that he was far more than an aeronautical engineer.
He was the former director of the supersonic wind tunnel
at Guidonia, thirty miles from Rome, which was the largest of its kind in the world. Ferri had experimented with
speeds of almost twenty-five-hundred miles an hour, a level
untouched by any other nation at the time. To Berg, Ferri's name thus began to suggest faster planes and control of
the skies.

Germany had already begun the production of jet
planes and was edging closer to manned aircraft capable of
breaking the sound barrier. Germany, as well as Britain,
was expending huge sums and energy on supersonic flight.
The United States paled in comparison.

English and Russian secret agents had offered Ferri lucrative and sensitive posts in their war machines, but he
had declined. Berg learned further that Ferri was a marked
man. Germany — its once indomitable Luftwaffe losing
supremacy — was offering a huge reward for Ferri's capture. Nazi patrols, accompanied by SS intelligence officers,
combed large areas north of Rome in search of the scientist.

Berg was determined to find Ferri. He eventually located Ferri's mother-in-law, Signora Gina Mola, who lived

on Via Palestro in Rome. She confided in Moe that Ferri was in the Apennine Mountains in the Camerino region, some one hundred and fifty miles north of Rome, an area still in Nazi hands. Berg decided to risk the journey. Ferri was worth it.

Moe's trip northward was accomplished by an army jeep and Italian partisans. They skirted German patrols and scoured the region for more than a week.

Unable to locate Ferri, the unit brought Berg to Florence, where he planned to enter the German-held and operated Galileo Works to determine if the munitions plant was developing new weaponry, possibly rockets, as reported to intelligence. Moe spent several days in the home of a partisan in Florence's Rifredi section studying dossiers on Galileo. He then burned the papers. In the privacy of his room he read a German book aloud to sharpen his guttural enunciations. At the dinner table on the day he chose to enter Galileo, Moe thanked his hosts and raised a glass of red wine in toast, then left the modest home dressed as a German army officer. He carried papers identifying him as a member of the general staff in Berlin. His hair was crew cut; his tall boots handsomely black under a bemedaled uniform, and he carried a swagger stick. Moe Berg entered Galileo receiving salutes from German soldiers. He observed production lines as he moved arrogantly slow, enduring critical glances from assembly workers. The catcher then conferred with plant managers and reportedly emphasized Berlin was not satisfied with production. One plant official, according to a secret report, was cooperating with the Allies and privately informed Berg that no new types of weapons were being manufactured. Moe's report to Washington also noted, "The conference was interrupted several times by the burst of artillery fire overhead."

In August, Moe learned that Antonio Ferri had returned to Rome. The pair met in Berg's apartment.

"Moe asked me a lot of questions about my work at Guidonia aeronautical laboratory, where I was in charge of the high-speed wind tunnel," Ferri states. "We had a very advanced supersonic facility there, and I told him Italy and Germany were far ahead of the United States in high-speed flight.

"I also told him that others, including Englishmen, were after me to accept jobs in their countries. I informed him of the premium the Germans had out for my capture."

Berg cabled John Stack, an official of the National Advisory Committee on Aeronautics in Washington, citing Ferri's credentials. An immediate reply from Dr. Jerome C. Hunsacker, NACA director, asked Berg to deliver Ferri to the United States at once.

Ferri, however, declined the invitation with regret, stressing that his priority was to fight for his homeland. "That was a rough period in my life," Ferri says. "I had been fighting with the Spartico Division, a group of resistance fighters. My father, Italian Supreme Court Justice Giovanni Battista, and my two brothers, Guiseppe, a professor at the University of Rome, and Licinio, were founding members of the group.

"We had been engaged in hit-and-run tactics against the Nazis. We bombed bridges so the Germans would have difficulty moving out of areas before the Allies arrived.

"I was very depressed with what I had seen happening

in Italy. I told Moe I was not interested in technical work at the time. I went back to the mountains."

After Paris was liberated in late August, Berg went to France to interview atomic scientists. His primary objective was Frédéric Joliot, famous French physicist who was married to Irene Curie, daughter of Madame Marie Curie, discoverer of radium. Joliot, who remained in France during the war, had a political profile that ranged, according to baffled American intelligence agents, from pro-Nazi leanings to communist sympathies.

A Nobel Prize winner, Joliot concerned himself with uranium fission. He produced the first chain reaction of uranium atoms, although it, unlike the subsequent Fermi test, was not self-sustaining and quickly died out. Joliot also had hoped to explode a uranium bomb for his country in the Sahara but this was abandoned when Germany overran France.

A secret government report recorded that Berg met Joliot at his laboratory at the College of France in Paris. Joliot told Moe that several of Hitler's atomic scientists visited his laboratory and conducted experiments on his cyclotron, a vital apparatus used for smashing atoms. Berg elicited from Joliot the types of experiments the Germans conducted on the cyclotron. He told Berg Germany was years away from perfecting atomic weapons. Berg cabled this projection to Washington.

Aside from his scientific responsibilities, Berg chronicled Nazi war crimes for Donovan. The growing revelations of atrocities pierced the athlete, and, when he visited, with other OSS officers, Pope Pius XII at the Vatican after the liberation of Rome, Moe, speaking in Italian, urged the pontiff to speak out against the genocide. Scientists and others detailed for Moe offenses committed by Hermann Goering, Joachim von Ribbentrop, Martin Bormann, Heinrich Himmler, Julius Streicher, Ernest Kaltenbrunner, and Fritz Sauckel. General Donovan, two years later, assisted in their prosecution at the Nuremberg trials. Moe, in an apparent unofficial capacity, witnessed those historic trials.

Compilation of the horror stories in Germany added to the already heavy burden of endless hours of investigations and confrontations that challenged Berg's stamina. But there were victories to appease weariness. In early September, he again met with Antonio Ferri.

"I was still depressed," Ferri recalls, "and Moe asked me again if I would go to the United States. This time, I agreed to go for three months."

Stringent immigration guidelines, however, deterred Ferri's immediate departure. Incensed at these strictures, Donovan and Berg asked President Roosevelt to intervene. The President reacted favorably and reportedly told aides, "I see Berg is still catching pretty well."

OSS agent and author Peter Tompkins, based in Rome, was directed to accompany Ferri to America:

"I was told, 'We've got to get Ferri to the United States.' I was given a letter which said to get him there because President Roosevelt wanted him.

"We left from Caserta Air Force Base in Naples for Casablanca, where we stayed overnight. I was robbed of my money at the hotel. We flew out of Casablanca for New

York, but were unable to land there and had to go to Newark, New Jersey, instead.

"It was four in the morning. One customs guy asked, referring to Ferri, 'Who's this?' Ferri had brought along a huge trunk filled with paraphernalia. There must have been four hundred pounds of material in the trunk. I showed the customs guy the letter I had and told him I was delivering Ferri for General Donovan. The customs guy took one look at the letter and said, 'Okay. Okay.' "

Ferri was taken to Langley Field in Virginia, where he lectured and arranged courses in aeronautics. His theories and experiments in high-speed flight baffled the National Advisory Committee on Aeronautics engineers. According to one report, "The people at Langley thought he was crazy."

It became apparent, however, that Ferri's work was superior to America's efforts in supersonic flight, and he was asked to stay in the country after his three months expired.

"I told them no," Ferri recalls. "My family was still in Italy. I wanted to see them. I said I would remain if they could be brought to America." NACA officials acted promptly so that Ferri's wife, Renata, and children, Paolo, Roselle and Joseph, could join him.

"While they were in Rome, Moe helped them prepare for the trip," Ferri continues. "He had become a good friend. And he was instrumental in assisting them in entering this country."

Dr. Ferri now heads the New York University Aerospace Laboratory. His contributions in high-speed flight theory ushered in the era of supersonic aircraft. On the basis of Ferri's work, in conjunction with that of others, Charles E.

Yeager flew the rocket-powered Bell X–1 on October 14, 1947, and broke the sound barrier. This marked the first time manned aircraft rushed beyond the speed of sound in level flight.

Of Moe's efforts in persuading Ferri to come to America, Dix wrote, "Mr. Berg's recognition of Dr. Ferri's worth and the full report on him was of exceptional value and assistance to our government. Dr. Ferri saved this Government at least two years in very important development work and many dollars that our Government would otherwise have spent in development work."

Berg's efforts in Italy received special recognition. A coterie of grateful people in science, education, and government asked the University of Rome to honor him. A Doctor of Laws degree was conferred upon him on September 11, 1944, by the university. The citation reads: "This academic community, in a spirit of grateful recognition of our liberation by the Allied Armies of England and the United States of America in the year just past, bestows with fond salutation, the Title of Doctor of Laws upon Morris Berg, truly distinguished Patron of Legal Science. He is eminently deserving of this Honor by reason of his talented and humane dedication to the noble task of the Restoration and renewal of this venerable and highly esteemed Institution — a perennial source of Academic Excellence."

One of Berg's ancillary responsibilities during the war was to research German biological and chemical warfare. The Allies, victories mounting, were worried that Germany might use poison gas as a countermeasure. Intelligence on this threat remained a high priority.

Moe probed all the possibilities that Germany might be planning to deploy X-rays and gamma rays in radiological warfare. These radioactive poisons, some scientists believed, might be produced as by-products from atomic bomb experiments. The radioactive material, Moe learned, could be contained in an ordinary bomb and dropped, spewing poison on Allied troops.

Berg's investigations led him to Switzerland and France, where he interrogated university chemists and officials of major industries who did research on poison gas. He also questioned captured German officers to determine if they knew whether their military leaders ever discussed plans to use poison gas or other types of germ warfare. Also, Berg sought to learn the extent of the Axis reservoir of poison gas.

On the basis of his investigations, Berg informed Washington that the Germans "did not have an active, large scale or skilled operation on this subject." But he cautioned that his investigations were by no means conclusive and urged continued surveillance.

On a few occasions, Moe returned to Washington for conferences with military leaders to outline scientific developments in Europe. His stateside visits also afforded him the opportunity to watch baseball games. On these rare treats, Moe invariably ran into friends who had heard that he was in counterintelligence.

Red Smith, a sports columnist now with the *New York Times*, recalls meeting Moe at a ball game in Washington. Aware of Moe's reputation for being taciturn, Smith said in jest, "I understand, Moe, that you are in counterintelligence which, I assume, means that you are against intelligence."

Berg reacted by placing his index finger vertically over his lips, whispering, "Ssshhh," and then sticking out his hand, saying, "Nice to see you, Red."

Tom Yawkey remembers Berg's infrequent wartime appearances at Fenway Park: "I saw him a couple of times sitting out in the bleachers. The ushers recognized him and word would come to me. Moe never came to see me during those visits. I wondered if he was angry at me. I saw him after the war and said, 'Gee, Moe, how come you never dropped up to see me? I know you were here a couple of times to see ball games. Did I do something to hurt you?' He said, 'Gosh, no, Tom,' explaining that he had had so much on his mind that he could not talk. Not even to his closest friends. That is why he stayed away from his friends during this period."

7
Heisenberg

As THE YEAR 1944 APPROACHED ITS END, there were indications that victory in Europe and the Pacific could be realized within one year.

Rome and Paris had been liberated and the Allies were within German borders. American advances in the Pacific brought the war nearer to the Japanese mainland. Tokyo moved twenty thousand persons daily out of the city as aerial attacks doubled. And in the background, American and German scientists battled in laboratories to perfect the atomic bomb.

Moe Berg's efforts to unveil the German atomic bomb project became an obsession. He realized that only the bomb could reverse the course of the war, and was tormented by the dark prospects of a German success.

"Like all of us," said Calvert of the select cell of individuals involved in atomic spying, "Moe was obsessed with tracking down the German scientists and pinpointing the enemy's atomic bomb installations."

The key target was Herr Professor Werner Heisenberg, director of the Kaiser Wilhelm Institute for Physics in Berlin, recognized as one of the world's geniuses and Germany's foremost atomic scientist. Noted for his work on quantum theory, he founded quantum mechanics in 1925 and won fame for his "uncertainty principle," which states the impossibility of determining simultaneously the position and velocity of a particle. American intelligence indicated that he was working on the problem of separating the rare U-235 isotope from the more abundant U-238 and that he was the nucleus of the German atomic bomb program. Indeed, Heisenberg had stunned a supersecret meeting of Germany's foremost scientists and military men in Berlin, in 1942, by declaring that an atomic bomb, capable of annihilating a city, could be constructed, and its explosive device need not be larger than "a pineapple." But doubts persisted in the minds of certain Allied scientists that Heisenberg was willing to build an A-bomb and present it to Hitler. According to Professor Samuel Goudsmit, head of the scientific branch of the U.S. Alsos Mission, whose function was to capture enemy scientists, documents and atomic installations in the wake of Allied invasions, "One had always hoped Heisenberg was pro-American and strongly anti-Nazi."

Learning Heisenberg's political stance, therefore, was critical. If he were goldbricking and not amenable to building a bomb, the chances of an Allied victory seemed assured.

Moe was determined to reach Heisenberg, but he knew he could not enter Hechingen, where Heisenberg reportedly still lived and worked in late 1944. That area remained under Nazi control and was unsafe to penetrate.

The next best vantage point was Switzerland, a haven for informants on German science as well as the spy center of the war.

Moe traveled extensively in Switzerland. The small Alpine nation was a veritable proving ground for the stamina and guile of undercover agents. Geographically boxed in by Nazi-dominated countries during most of the war, its cities were infested with spies and counteragents, with and without portfolio. The atmosphere was charged with intrigue.

Moe's chief contact in Switzerland was Professor Scherrer, the country's leading experimental physicist, and a teacher at the Federal Institute of Technology in Zurich. Implacably anti-Nazi, Scherrer maintained contact throughout the war with German scientists who worked on atomic research and development. He was a fount of information for Moe.

According to Goudsmit, Berg and Scherrer became "close friends." Berg found the scientist to be a man of high principle. Unlike many people in academia who looked the other way, Scherrer placed his life in jeopardy by providing the United States with a portrait of German atomic scientists. Scherrer's revulsion for the Third Reich stemmed from his fear that the Wehrmacht might invade neutral Switzerland. He felt nothing was sacred to the plundering Nazi regime and that an Allied victory was necessary for the restoration of peace. He conveyed these feelings to Moe.

Berg became Scherrer's confidant, and on at least one occasion, Moe was able to assist Scherrer. In late 1944, Scherrer's stock of heavy water, which he needed to conduct further research on his laboratory cyclotron, ran out.

Goudsmit relates, "I had kept a small cylinder of heavy hydrogen in Strasbourg and I gave it to Moe and said, 'Bring that to our friend Scherrer, who needs it.' And Moe did it and that made Scherrer very happy. In turn, Scherrer helped us greatly."

Scherrer and Berg spent hours reviewing reports on Germany's atomic bomb project. The information supplied them came from a number of sources, including paid informants. Many of the reports were in conflict with one another. Some hinted that Hitler would soon unleash the most devastating weapon in the history of warfare. Other reports contended that Germany's atomic development was retarded.

By late 1944, Berg and Scherrer were at a virtual standstill in their quest to develop a clear picture of the enemy's progress. They agreed the best method of gathering the most accurate intelligence was the direct approach — face-to-face confrontations with Germany's top two atomic scientists, Heisenberg and Hahn.

Berg concocted schemes designed to lure the German scientists to Switzerland to lecture at the Federal Institute of Technology. In reporting one such attempt, a secret government document states, "Berg, through his arrangements in Switzerland, had a request sent to Hahn . . . to give a lecture in Switzerland. The invitation was delivered but Hahn could not give the lecture."

Surprisingly, Heisenberg accepted a similar invitation. This marked the first and only time Heisenberg left Germany since the United States declared war. It was one of the major espionage coups of World War II.

As Heisenberg recalled the event: "I went on the invitation by Scherrer because I had the impression it would be nice to go and keep connections with old friends. I knew Scherrer. He was an old friend."

When Berg was informed that the German professor had agreed to deliver a talk on December 18, he was prepared for anything — even, reportedly, the assassination of Heisenberg.

"Moe told me," remembers George Gloss, Boston rare-book dealer and a close friend, "that he was to find out whether the Germans were actually making progress with an atomic bomb and if Heisenberg was propelling this effort. If so, he told me he was to eliminate Heisenberg — kill him." This incident related by Gloss was the only revelation by Berg that researchers could elicit from among scores interviewed on the catcher's foreign assignments.

Gloss recalls being shaken by the story. "Being a pacifist, it shocked my Quaker sensibilities. I said, 'Moe, you don't mean you were going to kill Heisenberg, one of the world's greatest scientists?' Moe said, 'Yes. If it meant world survival.' But Moe prayed that he would not have to do it. He really did not want it to come to that."

However, Berg's own sensitivities, aside from whatever instructions he may have received concerning Heisenberg, were increasingly affected by the atrocities on the Continent. Millions had died and millions more would follow if Hitler's dream of world conquest succeeded. And, intelligence reports emphasized, Heisenberg — more than any other German atomic physicist — had the genius to deliver the bomb. There was no doubt of that. The real questions remained: was Germany on the verge of having the bomb and was Heisenberg its architect?

The fateful day arrived. Berg, according to Groves,

passed himself off as a student and obtained a seat in the lecture hall. Goudsmit believes Moe "probably" got the seat "through Scherrer." Security in the room and around the building was tight, befitting Heisenberg's position in German science. Swiss police guarded entrances to the institute and lecture hall, while SS agents permeated the area. The institute reflected, however, an atmosphere of academic calm.

Berg displayed his admittance letter to sentries and walked into the lecture room. There was no check for firearms. Security did not detect Moe's shoulder holster containing a Beretta. There were twenty persons in the classroom, several of them pro-Nazi scientists, Berg later related in a cable to Washington.

Moe took his seat in the front row. Heisenberg, facing his audience, was only feet away from America's foremost atomic spy. "I did not know that Moe Berg was in the room," Heisenberg later said. "I never met him."

Moe followed the lecture in German, the spoken language of the region.

"I do not recall the title of my talk," Heisenberg says. "But it was philosophical. Quantum theory. I had told Scherrer I would not talk about anything political." Heisenberg's talk ran true to his prescribed intentions: pure, basic, unadulterated physics. There were no Freudian slips, no lapses into the problems of separating U-235 from U-238. Heisenberg did not mention heavy water or atomic reactors. He made no disclosure of Germany's progress on the atomic bomb.

Heisenberg was probably unaware that a German was in his audience clinically diagnosing his talk. In his report to

Washington, Berg said a German scientist was in the class-room "for the direct purpose of watching Heisenberg and reporting back to Hitler's headquarters the general infor-mation of the lecture."

Heisenberg's innocent presentation completed, the au-dience parted into small, informal discussion groups. Much of these conversations focused on the war, Hitler, German scientists, and their research.

Berg moved in his graceful, quiet style from one group to another. He heard one of the German scientists main-tain that "Hitler was healthy and working hard." This contradicted rumors in Germany that suggested Hitler had suffered a nervous breakdown and had never recovered from the foiled July 20 assassination plot. Berg was able to corroborate, through loose talk, that many of the main German scientists were in southern Germany and that the heart of the German research laboratories was centered there.

Moe inched his way closer to Heisenberg, who stood chatting with another physicist near the blackboard. He pretended to study the equations scribbled on the black-board as he came within earshot of Heisenberg. His ears were pricked — sensitive antennae attuned to pick up any critical information from the mouth of the preeminent German scientist.

"One of the expressions Moe overheard," according to Dr. Goudsmit, "was Heisenberg saying, 'Well, we are los-ing this war, but how nice it would have been if Germany had won it.'"

That night Scherrer gave a dinner party at his home for the visiting German, which Moe Berg attended. Heisenberg remembers the invitation and the admonition he delivered to the Swiss physicist: "I told Scherrer I would go to his home on one condition: that no politics be discussed. But there were political questions and I answered them indirectly. I said I did not believe Gemany could win the war, but I couched my statements."

Berg left the party and cabled the German scientist's defeatist remarks to OSS headquarters in Washington. The report was sent to General Groves, who went to the White House immediately to apprise President Roosevelt. The President, ailing and in the last months of his life, shook hands with Groves and said, "Fine, just fine. Let us pray Heisenberg is right. And, General, my regards to the catcher."

British Prime Minister Winston Churchill was also briefed on Heisenberg's statements, which served as powerful indicators that Germany was having problems with building an atomic bomb and would not be able to produce one in time to bail out Hitler and his crumbling empire. The news brought relief to the Manhattan Project scientists, who had continued to worry about the German effort. Official concern over the enemy's atomic activity did not lessen, because the possibility loomed that Heisenberg had deliberately misled his listeners by planting false information. History, however, shows that Heisenberg told the truth.

In writing of the classroom incident and its aftermath, Lieutenant Colonel Dix stated, "The risks taken by Mr. Berg at the lecture and in the discussions after and coming out with the desired information from the highest German authority were of wonderful help to this government."

When Heisenberg returned home two days after the lecture, he faced difficulties: "The Gestapo had made a record of my visit and I was in trouble when I got back to Germany. There was talk of high treason. However, Walther Gerlach, head of the German atomic energy project, smoothed things over for me."

But Heisenberg's troubles were not over. Berg learned through German scientists who had fled to Switzerland that Hitler had been displeased with Heisenberg and "made it very uncomfortable" for him, a secret U.S. government report stated. The document added that Berg was informed that "at times Heisenberg did not give to Hitler all of the information developed" on the atomic bomb. This reinforced belief among some Allied leaders that the renowned atomist was politically anti-Nazi but strongly pronationalist, an attitude shared by some other major German scientists, many of whom remained in Germany for various reasons, not excluding the fact that they received special considerations.

Berg remained in Switzerland, where he secretly confronted other German scientists and government officials who supported Heisenberg's political and military beliefs. According to a secret government report, "Approximately December 31, 1944, Mr. Berg learned the Germans felt that successful developments would require two years."

In addition, Moe learned from the Germans that Kikuchi and Yukawa were the main Japanese atomic scientists, and that Kapitza, Yoffee, Fredericks and Frank were the top Russians.

Moe at times pursued people for days in his intelligence missions. One instance involved a Nazi-leaning Swiss professor, Dallenbach, who reportedly was collaborating with the Germans on an important atomic project. Moe hounded Dallenbach throughout Switzerland, following the scientist into cafés, lecture halls and railroad coaches. To ward off any suspicion, Moe often wore disguises. He blended in anonymously on the crowded streets of Zurich dressed as one of the thousands of faceless refugees who had streamed into Switzerland from Italy, France, and Germany. Once, his hair powdered white, Moe followed Dallenbach into the private library of a University of Zurich professor. Berg sat at the same table with Dallenbach, ostensibly preoccupied with a stack of engineering manuals. Reporting on this incident, which occurred in early 1945, a secret government document stated, "Mr. Berg noted books and pages on which Dallenbach was working and when the books were replaced, he learned that Dallenbach was investigating the history of the atomic topic." Berg's investigations ultimately disclosed that Dallenbach was building a cyclotron in Bisingen, the government report noted. The report stated that Berg was informed Dallenbach's cyclotron "was running in a small successful fashion." This development prompted Manhattan Project officials to want to know more about Dallenbach's atom-smashing machine, and the catcher's probing reached fruition when, in the words of the secret report, he "assisted in obtaining" duplicates of drawings and a description of the Swiss scientist's cyclotron. The material, the report added, was "specially sent to General Groves and Dr. Bush [Vannevar Bush, chairman of the Office of Scientific Research and Development] by General Donovan."

The manner in which Berg stole these vital documents is unknown.

About this same time, Moe was again advised that most of the main German atomic scientists were in Hechingen, Bisingen and Ringingen, all south of Stuttgart. Despite the contentions of Heisenberg and other important scientists, Berg still harbored concern, in February 1945, that Germany could unleash an atomic bomb built in laboratories functioning in these three highly protected villages. He recommended "that these areas should be thoroughly bombed, if that met with headquarters war strategy," according to the government report. After studying the proposal, those privy to the atomic picture rejected the recommendation, apparently believing, as they had earlier, that bombing would drive German laboratories deeper underground.

Berg's secret wartime missions enhanced his innate mysteriousness. If he met friends in foreign capitals, he would brush past them muttering firm apologies. Don Griffin, a Princeton classmate who was with the Air Transport Command during the war, recalls seeing Moe in Africa. "He recognized me but did not want anybody to associate the two of us. He said, 'If I don't speak to you don't be surprised because I don't want to be recognized.' "

This detachment — partly natural and partly fostered by the exigencies of espionage — created an added mystique. Intelligence personnel began talking in awe about this big man dressed in black who looked like an undertaker.

Dr. Goudsmit, now at Brookhaven National Laboratory on Long Island, remembers his first meeting with Berg. "I think I first met him in Paris or Göttingen. I do not re-

member the details. Something had fallen into our hands
and we were waiting for other people to join us and somebody said a military plane was coming in with two air force
people and with a civilian — Moe Berg, whom I had heard
of but never had met before. He had been described to me
and he showed up exactly as described. He refused to wear
a uniform. He was in his black suit and black hat, exactly
as always and never changed. Somewhat like a character
out of a book."

When the Allies took Göttingen, Germany, Moe went
there to carry out investigations of German high-speed experimental work. He worked with members of the U.S.
Alsos team. John Stack, chief of NACA's high-speed experimentation program at Langley Field, reported that
Moe's trip to Göttingen with Russell G. Robinson, an
NACA aerodynamicist attached to the Alsos mission, "was
most helpful." Stack, according to a secret government
document, reported that "the trip produced the collection
of approximately 80 per cent of the information of the
German development work on high speed aeronautical designs and tests."

Robinson, now retired director of Aeronautics and
Flight Mechanics at the National Aeronautics and Space
Administration's Ames Research Center in Moffett Field,
California, remembers that the seized documents were
labeled "secret" and "top secret," and included informa-
tion on the "swept-wing" principle:

"I was impressed with the German work on the revolutionary concept of swept wings for easing flight into and
through the speed of sound. The amount and importance

of the German documents was clear, doubly so because the same kind of thinking and research, theoretical and early experimental, was going on independently and secretly at NACA's Langley Laboratory. Dr. Robert T. Jones, now of NASA's Ames Research Center, was responsible in this country for the concept and its mathematical basis. His ideas, which I knew of, were reported in the spring of 1945.

"The documents were expedited to the United States because of their importance in corroborating and adding additional experimental data to speed the application of this principle to American aircraft.

"The application of the German swept-wing principle may now be seen every day on Boeing 747s, 727s, 707s and B-52s, Lockheed 1011s, Douglas DC-10s, DC-8s and F-101s, North American Sabre-Jets, F-100s, etc."

Robinson cannot recall Berg's precise role in the seizure of the documents, but states, "I'm not surprised that he was involved because he impressed me with his utter discretion, that is, he did not discuss his activities. I probably did not know at the time his official capacity.

"Moe struck me as extremely intelligent, original in his thinking, highly motivated and self-propelled. He was completely devoted to his mission. I was intrigued at the time that a professional baseball player would be so effective in this totally different sphere of activity."

Not everyone was intrigued with Berg. Moe found an unexpected problem in Switzerland in the person of Allen Dulles, director of the spy network in that country for the United States. Their relationship was a stormy one. Berg, carrying the highest authorization of his government and

acting autonomously, would not relent to Dulles's de-
mands that he report his activities.

Casey says, "I guess most of the people who could tell
you about this would say Moe got into a helluva row with
Allen Dulles. Moe didn't want to tell Allen what he was
up to and Allen didn't want anyone around who wouldn't
tell him."

Moe was not the only man having trouble with Dulles.
Donovan apparently also had a falling-out with the future
CIA director. Whether Moe's difficulties with Dulles had
any bearing on Donovan's feelings about the spy chief of
Switzerland is not known. Donovan rejected a promotion
recommendation that would have given Dulles overall
command of the OSS in the European Theater. Dulles
subsequently assumed the lesser role as OSS chief in occupied Germany. Another indication that there were ill feelings between the two was graphically presented by Berg
when he related to his friend, Edward "Ted" Sanger, that
had Donovan known Allen Dulles was an honorary pall-
bearer at the general's funeral in February 1959, "Bill
would have jumped out of his coffin."

Despite the differences between Berg and Dulles, also a
Princeton alumnus, there were thaws in their chilly relationship. Dulles helped Moe on some of his missions. One
notable instance was in early 1945 after Berg discovered
that the Germans planned to build a supercyclotron in
Bisingen. Berg cabled Washington that he understood the
Germans wanted to use the atom-smashing machine to
separate an isotope, possibly of thorium. He stated that the
I. G. Farben company, a huge chemical combine in Germany, was building the cyclotron. I. G. Farben had been

allocated large sums of money to produce war matériel. Its plant at Merseburg had made synthetic gasoline and other war products. The company had also been engaged in manufacturing heavy water. In 1944 alone, over one million Reichsmarks had been provided for the company's heavy water operations at the Leuna Works, Merseburg. The firm, along with several others in Germany, was deeply involved in uranium research.

Berg's memorandum to Washington mentioned that "some surprises" could develop from the supercyclotron Farben planned to build. Berg sought to send a spy into Bisingen with the help of one of Dulles's aides, Gerhard Van Arkel. A Washington labor lawyer and former general counsel of the National Labor Relations Board, Van Arkel was in Bern when Moe, then in Annemasse, France, near the Swiss border, contacted him.

As Van Arkel relates it, "We had a house at Annemasse where we used to keep people we were smuggling in and out of Switzerland. Moe sent me a message and said he would like to talk with me. I went to see him at Annemasse and he told me that he was charged with a very important mission that President Roosevelt was informed about, General Donovan personally approved of and Whitney Shepardson, who was in charge of Secret Intelligence of OSS, was behind. He said this project involved getting a man into southern Germany, and could I help him get this man in. I didn't ask him what this man's mission was and he didn't volunteer to tell me."

After some soul-searching, Van Arkel balked at the plan. "I told Moe I was against the plan. I explained to him that I had a group I was working with in Basel. It was largely pro-Allied Swiss with perhaps several Germans. They had been providing some useful information for some months. But I told Moe I had always operated under the strictest of rules never to infiltrate someone from the outside into my group. I did not feel it was wise to do this.

"Moe again insisted on the top priority of this mission but I remained against it. Then he got in touch with Allen Dulles, who started to twist my arm. After considerable hesitation and a lot of misgivings I agreed to do it, but on one condition — that I alone would give Moe's agent his instructions."

Moe's plan was to have his operative enter Bisingen disguised as a Russian slave laborer, since American aerial photos revealed slave labor camps had been built there in late 1944.

Van Arkel explains the plan further:

"We had bribed a frontier guard near Geneva so we could get people across that border without difficulty. So I went over to see this fellow Moe had brought with him. I told him he was to take the trolley car from Annemasse to near the Swiss border, then to walk down a path to the frontier and I'd alert this guard so he could get across the Swiss border. Then he was to go to Geneva and take a certain train to Basel and he was to get off the train at Basel, walk down the street and — with certain recognition signals, a peaked cap and newspaper folded under his arm — he would meet a man there who could give him a passport to use.

"The next thing I learned was that the Swiss police had arrested both of them, Moe's agent and the head of my group."

Van Arkel said he later heard from another source that

Berg was on the same train as his agent, three or four seats behind him, and had unknowingly been followed by Swiss counterintelligence agents.

"I heard Moe was fearful something might go wrong," Van Arkel said, in explaining why Berg was on the same train. "Obviously the Swiss counterintelligence knew Moe. He had been in and out of our offices all the time and, I think, under pretty strict surveillance. And, when they got to Basel, the Swiss counterintelligence intervened to pick them up." Berg escaped arrest because he carried a passport granting him diplomatic immunity.

Later, Berg established that the Germans had jettisoned plans for the atom-smashing machine. In a cable to Washington, he said he had received reports that "one of the main German scientists who had conceived the idea of a supercyclotron was overruled by the others."

Van Arkel recalls dining with Moe on several occasions. "I had the notion he traveled around a good bit, but nobody knew exactly what the hell he was up to. I did, at the time, see the cables, with few exceptions, that went through our office. And I saw the cables that Moe was sending from Zurich and other spots around Switzerland. His cables were Greek to me. They were full of terms which at the time didn't mean a damned thing to me; terms such as isotopes and thorium and uranium and so forth. I hadn't the vaguest inkling of what was going on, but after I'd heard about the atomic bombs being dropped on Japan and had read the reports on them, I understood what Moe had been doing — that is, counterintelligence on the A-bomb."

Moe's missions had their lighter moments, too. Colonel Russell Forgan, OSS commander in the European Theater

and now a prominent New York investment banker, remembers visiting a front-line hospital in Germany with
Berg and Donovan. "Moe and I accompanied Donovan,"
recalls Forgan. "We went to this front-line hospital where
a reporter by the name of Allen was. [Major Robert S.
Allen, who, during peacetime, was columnist Drew Pear-
son's partner.] Allen had been wounded. Bill wanted to
see him because they were good friends. While Bill went in
to see Allen, Moe and I stayed outside because we didn't
know him and there was no reason for us to go in there.

"We were sitting on a grassy bank overlooking a small
open area when a couple of GI's came out of the hospital. I
guess they were hospital attendants. They had baseball
gloves and a ball and started throwing the ball back and
forth. Moe was watching them and he turned to me
and said, 'Do you think I could interrupt those fellows and
catch a ball a few times?' I'd guess he hadn't caught a ball
in, I don't know how long. I said, 'Sure you can.'

"Moe went down and said, 'Look, do you fellows mind if
I catch with you?' The guy with a catcher's mitt said, 'Sure.
Take this.' He handed Moe the mitt. So Moe put it on and
started throwing the ball with that short, quick flip, like
that, you know. And this kid, the one who had given him
the catcher's mitt, kept looking at the way Moe threw the
ball. The kid kept looking and looking and looking and
said, 'Hell, I know who you are. The last time I saw you
was in Sportsman's Park. You're Moe Berg.' And Moe
came back and, boy, he was the happiest guy. Imagine, the
middle of Germany with a war going on and this guy recognized him. It pleased him tremendously."

Moe was not always pleased at being identified. Dr. Berg

recalls Moe telling him that his inclination was toward total anonymity. "It would have been highly unusual during the war if Moe had walked through large cities of England, France, Switzerland and Italy without being recognized by any of the thousands of soldiers who had seen him play on the several teams of the American League, or who knew him personally.

"Anyway, when this did happen, and say the meeting took place in France, Moe would deny the identification and talk hurriedly in idiomatic French and walk away. If in Italy, in idiomatic Italian. If in England, with an Oxford accent.

"The greatest difficulty he had was when someone would yell behind his back, 'Hey, Moe,' and he would have to remember that he was not Moe Berg and that he must not under any circumstances respond to the call of his name."

Berg's mode of travel provided a continuing source of intrigue among his superiors. Moe had never learned to drive, telling friends, "I hate the bureaucracy of the automobile. Forms, rules, licenses. I don't have time for that sort of madness." So, upon occasion, he hitchhiked and walked long distances on critical assignments. Whitney Shepardson, the first OSS chief of Secret Intelligence in London, and General Donovan often professed amazement at how Moe traveled to assignments. Relating their curiosity to friends years later, they referred to Moe as "World War II's most prolific hitchhiker."

Moe's disdain for the automobile was heightened by a near fatal incident that occurred in early 1944 in occupied France. A member of the French underground was to drive Moe to the small village of Héricourt in eastern

France, near the Swiss border. Moe had made arrangements to confer with a German scientist who was collaborating with the Allies. Midway during the trip through the
meandering countryside a light snow intensified. The car
failed to climb a hill, and, after remaining in the halted
vehicle for an indefinite period during the early evening,
the pair decided to seek refuge. The alternative, they felt,
was freezing to death. Moe, dressed as a native Frenchman,
wore a black coat, and his driver wrapped a blanket
around himself as they struggled through snow and darkness that covered the road. They inched through an un-
ending field of whiteness. Their gait was slowed further by
a cruel wind that joined the swirling snow that reached
their waists. They locked arms to stay together, breaking
their hold only to brush snow and ice from their raw faces
and eyebrows. Their legs were virtually frozen after two
hours. They lost confidence they were on the Héricourt
road, and there were no stars to guide the catcher. Their
pain increased, as did the danger of death by freezing, but
they groped on. They moaned in their anguish, eyes straining to see. Approximately four miles and three hours from
their starting point, the unfriendly barking of dogs greeted
them. They stood beside a small, snow-covered country
home and its owner opened the door.

Relating the incident after the war, Professor Scherrer
assessed, "Moe and his driver were more dead than alive."

In the spring of 1945, as the death knell for the Third
Reich started to ring, General Groves ordered Moe to devote all his time to determining if Germany's main atomic
scientists were still living in the Hechingen-Bisingen area.

In his memoirs, Groves states that by the end of April "our principal concern at this point was to keep information and atomic scientists from falling into the hands of the Russians."

Groves and others aware of the forthcoming historic era knew atomic energy would play the deciding role in the balance of power. The top German scientists were highly prized objects and could be of tremendous help to Russia. If seized by the Russians, they could, in time, build an atomic bomb for Stalin, nullifying any advantage the United States would have in the postwar period.

Berg's reports to Manhattan Project officials reconfirmed that the cream of Germany's atomic corps remained in the villages of the Black Forest. As Allied armies stormed through southern Germany, the Alsos team, in the wake of the invasions, plucked up Hitler's main scientists, some in small groups, others individually. All of the top ten enemy scientists were seized, except Heisenberg. Efforts to capture him redoubled and, finally, on May 3, he was arrested in Urfeld in the Bavarian Alps.

The seizure of these scientists represented a major coup for the United States in what signaled the beginning of the massive hunt for German scientists by Russia and America. Berg's detailed reports on the whereabouts of the brains behind the German atomic effort allowed American investigators to capture them.

8
Meitner

Soon after Heisenberg's capture, Moe Berg entered Sweden to meet the preeminent physicist Dr. Lise Meitner, who was then living in Stockholm. He went there to determine if Germany were capable of engineering a last-minute surprise in atomic weaponry. Key Groves aide Robert Furman said, "We were concerned about the German bomb effort right to the very end."

Dr. Meitner was credited with having explained how the atom had been split. For years she had worked with the German chemists Otto Hahn and Fritz Strassman, at the Kaiser Wilhelm Institute in Berlin, where the trio experimented in splitting the atom.

Dr. Meitner, a native of Austria, was part Jewish. In 1938, the Germans overran Austria, bringing her into Nazi hands. With the help of friends, she fled Germany and went to Stockholm. One day, Hahn wrote to her describing an experiment that had left him puzzled.

He had fired slow-speed neutrons at the uranium nucleus only to discover it produced an "atomic ghost" that should not have been there. Mathematically, Dr. Meitner, with the help of her gifted nephew, Dr. O. R. Frisch, deduced that Hahn had achieved one of the great discoveries in science: the splitting of the atom. In a paper on the event, Dr. Frisch added a new word to the lexicon — "fission." The Hahn experiment opened the way for exploitation of the tremendous energy of the uranium atom.

Meitner and Hahn continued corresponding with one another during the war. It was for this reason that Berg traveled to Stockholm to see her, hoping to learn what she knew about German atomic development.

According to Dix, "The Germans . . . kept in very close touch with Dr. Meitner and she was personally acquainted with the main German scientists on nuclear physics and knew their work from the historical point of view and pretty much of the up-to-date development."

Dix added: "It must be borne in mind that Miss Meitner was under German surveillance all the time in Sweden and, frankly, how Mr. Berg ever accomplished visiting her without being incarcerated, I do not know."

In describing how Berg might have won the confidence of Dr. Meitner, Professor Goudsmit observes: "The important thing about Moe was his personality. He was a kind of mysterious man, but a level man. He was a man that did not talk — did not gossip — unless it served a purpose. Moe's greatest ability was that he understood people. People trusted him. He was able to put pieces of information together intelligibly. He moved easily among people."

The scene at Dr. Meitner's apartment has never been divulged in much detail. Overall it amounted to Moe arguing that world survival would be threatened if the Germans were preparing to unload an eleventh-hour super-weapon. He pleaded to know if such an effort was under way.

But Berg's appeal offended the famous scientist's sense of propriety. Reports said she countered with arguments that she was a scholar and not a weapons manufacturer; that she abhorred weapons of any kind. Moe urged that the realities of the atomic bomb had to be faced, that he must know the facts. Dr. Meitner detested the probing questions. She did not like spying. The clash of the two brilliant minds ended abruptly when Dr. Meitner asked Moe to leave her apartment.

Berg left, dejected and bitter, his mind unable to fathom her position. She was pro-Allied, yet she refused to reveal information that might have a direct bearing on whether or not the Allies won.

Dr. Goudsmit believes, "She kicked Moe out because she belonged to those people who believe that prying is immoral. When Moe tried to get her confidence by saying frankly what he was after, she clammed up. In fact, she gave me hell once, for he had probably used my name in getting to see her. She said to me, 'Who is that terrible man you sent to me?' She blamed me for that after the war."

Dr. Frisch recalls that his aunt "vaguely mentioned having been approached by someone, but didn't give any name."

The outcome of the visit was a distinct blow to Berg. Goudsmit thinks it was "his only rebuff" that he remembered.

A few days after Berg's encounter with Meitner, on May 8, Germany surrendered, burying for good any atomic bomb threat it had posed for the Allies.

The Alsos team now concentrated on capturing enemy atomic installations and uranium ore stockpiles before the Russians did.

Berg had reported in late December 1944 that the principal enemy facility was under a hill near Hechingen and had a church mounted on top of it to ward off any suspicion of its real nature. This installation was Heisenberg's laboratory. A secret government document said Berg's report "turned out to be correct, as one of the seizures directly after V-E Day was of an installation in the hill which had a church mounted on top of it."

Reports, including one from Berg, pinpointed areas where large reserves of uranium ore were located on the Continent. Members of the Alsos team, making blitzlike forays into southern France, Belgium, and Germany, captured tons of this material, which was later shipped to the United States.

9
The War Ends

ON AUGUST 14, 1945, Japan surrendered after two of its major cities— Hiroshima and Nagasaki — were devastated by atomic bombs. A wave of relief washed over a tired world, a world convulsed by two great conflicts within twenty-five years. For millions, it meant a "sentimental journey" home.

Moe Berg took a brief leave from his duties in Europe to escort Paul Scherrer to the United States. The Swiss physicist's itinerary included a visit with Albert Einstein at Princeton and conferences with American colleagues at Massachusetts Institute of Technology and California Institute of Technology.

The pair first stopped in New York City, where Moe called Michael Burke, who had been reassigned to the OSS office there.

"One of the things the professor wanted to see was the Stork Club," Burke said. "Moe, being a very secretive fellow, did not want to take him into the Stork Club for fear of being recognized. So I took him in and Moe stood in a doorway across the street. We had a drink at the bar and the professor walked all around the club observing people drinking and dancing, as though they were under a microscope and he was conducting a laboratory experiment on American social behavior."

During their visit with Einstein, Berg told the author of the *Theory of Relativity* that he had read his "Atomic War or Peace" article, which had been published in the *Atlantic Monthly*.

Moe was astonished as Einstein replied, "I read your baseball story, Mr. Berg, in the *Atlantic*, also. You teach me to catch and I'll teach you mathematics." Boston rare-book dealer George Gloss remembers that Moe delighted in retelling that story.

During their stay on the West Coast, Berg introduced Scherrer to additional facets of Americana. He took him to meet his old friend, Lefty O'Doul, then manager of the San Francisco Seals in the Pacific Coast League. O'Doul invited them to view the game from the dugout — a rare treat, especially for a foreigner watching his first professional baseball game.

Ironically, while Moe, the atomic spy, was in America, his brother, Army Medical Corps Major Samuel Berg, was leading a medical team into Nagasaki to study the bomb's victims. Dr. Berg's Japan mission would yield a historical study of the effects of radioactive fallout on humans. "As I left for Japan, I had had no idea that Moe was an atomic spy," Dr. Berg recalls.

Samuel Berg, an internist, had been selected to head the Nagasaki medical unit because of his work in research pathology and hematology. For three years he had been assigned to the large research laboratory unit located in Hollandia in the Southwest Pacific. When the war ended, he was assigned to Manila to establish the Southwest Pacific Blood Bank.

Commenting on his Nagasaki mission, Dr. Berg says:

"We were to study the effects of the atomic bomb on the victims over a period of six weeks.

"We flew into Nagasaki six weeks after the bomb was dropped. My impression of Nagasaki was that it was horrible to realize that an entire city could be wiped out with just one bomb.

"Our main function was hematology. We made blood studies on the victims, noting the effects on the skin, the hair and development of jaundice."

Before his medical unit's six weeks had ended, Dr. Berg asked for an extension to study the effects on humans of radioactive fallout from an atomic explosion.

"Radioactive fallout was a new term to me because I had not read about the fallout at Alamogordo, New Mexico, where the first atomic bomb test was conducted.

"Some sheep and cows had been affected by the fallout from that test and that was the first time scientists realized the wind would carry some of the radioactive elements towards the ground and contaminate the food supply and the water supply."

Dr. Berg was granted an extra two weeks to conduct his study. That study proved persons living miles away from the area where the bomb was dropped could have died or suffered illness from the radiation.

Dr. Berg's clinical paper on his investigations constituted the first study on the effects of radioactive fallout on humans. The historical achievement was noted in newspapers throughout the world. Dr. Berg was cited for his work in the published history of New Jersey medicine called *The Healing Art*.

While Dr. Berg was in Japan, Moe received a letter from Whitney H. Shepardson, head of OSS Secret Intelligence. The letter requested Moe to chronicle his activities as an undercover agent. According to Otto Doering, a friend of Shepardson's, the chief of secret intelligence planned to write a book on the spy organization. Shepardson was interested in Berg's exploits and modus operandi.

The Shepardson letter, written on Office of Strategic Services stationery and dated August 9, 1945, reads:

Dear Moe:

I know that your plans have been changed recently and I may not have a chance to talk with you at length before you leave, since I am going on Saturday for a short vacation, and I gather that you may have left the country by the time I get back.

With regard to what you are going to do abroad, you will, of course, get your guidance from the same quarters from which you have received it before.

Before you go, however, I would very much appreciate your setting down in narrative form an account of what you have done over the period of the last year or fifteen months in connection with AZUSA [an OSS atomic code name]. I have been amazed at the detail which our policy makers have decided to give out. That, however, is none of my business. I am concerned with the fact that until now, and perhaps for some time to come, we are precluded from making any statement of the part which OSS has played for many months in this mat-

ter. We are entitled to claim credit at the appropriate time for
our contribution and that contribution has been very largely
through you. I don't believe there is anyone in the organization who can make this record correctly and in detail except
yourself and I, therefore, strongly hope that you will undertake this assignment and finish it before you leave.

It goes without saying that no part of any such material
would be published without all proper clearances and it might
very well be that even after clearance, the form of presentation
would be changed. But what concerns me is that from the first
available moment after the announcement of the atomic
bomb your part of the OSS record should be set down on
paper.

Please make it full rather than skimpy. Please add details
rather than leave them out. You might follow something of
the following pattern —

1. The lead.
2. Where you got it.
3. How you made contact.
4. How you developed relations.
5. What you learned.
6. What documentary material you acquired.
7. What you did with it.
8. Any estimate of the importance of this intelligence in the
   whole collection of that which was gathered together.
9. What further leads you got arising out of your relations
   with this person.

If this general pattern was followed in the case of one person after another whose relations with you are described, the
whole story would not only have a chronological sequence to
it, but it would also be set up with a certain unity and lastly it
would indicate the relationship between the personalities and
work of various individuals with each other.

If I fail to see you before I go, I want to say once again how
highly we value the work which you have done in this connec-

tion and how much it has meant to the organization that you have been working for on this revolutionary subject.

Sincerely yours,
Whitney H. Shepardson

Whether Berg responded to the request is not known, nor is it likely that it will ever come to light if he did. According to Doering, Shepardson later gave up attempts to do a book on the intelligence agency primarily because much of the material in Washington remained classified at that time. Shepardson later burned all the material he had on the subject.

Berg returned to Europe to chart a new course in counterintelligence — spying on the Russians. While most of the world sank back into womblike security, Russia was busy laying the groundwork for a different kind of war — a Cold War featuring nuclear blackmail. Lieutenant Colonel Calvert describes the change in the Russian attitude:

"We had already picked up the top ten German atomic scientists and interned them at Farm Hall, England. We had won the prizes. The Russians, on the other hand, did not have an Alsos team like ours during the war; they did not have body snatchers, per se.

"All the Russians were doing was trying to win a war. We watched them move across fields. They lived off the land. They'd never bathed in four years. Never been paid in four years. They were interested only in daily survival and did not concern themselves with picking up German scientists."

But, Calvert continues, in the summer of 1945, reports

started leaking out of Communist-controlled Germany
that Russian teams were kidnapping German scientists and
taking them to Russia. "They were beginning to sift
through the ashes to get the bodies," Calvert said.

In October, Berg, Calvert and two others made a trip
through Russian-held regions of Austria, Czechoslovakia
and Germany to interrogate scientists in those areas who
might have some knowledge of what was going on: "We
were attempting to formulate a picture as to the extent of
Russian interest in German scientists."

The others making the trip, according to Calvert, were
Peter F. Oates, now a New York attorney, and William L.
Warner, presently an insurance broker from Portland,
Oregon.

The small party drove in an army jeep from Munich to
Salzburg. "We left from there the next morning and drove
to Vienna, the last half of the trip being through Russian
territory," Calvert recounts. "We stayed in Vienna for
three days. Moe interrogated several scientists there to determine if the Russians had talked to them and, if so, what
they discussed and what they were interested in."

The group encountered immediate problems. The Russians turned down Calvert's request for a pass to travel
between Vienna and Prague, which was all Russian-occu-
pied land. The Russian refusal forced the foursome to take
the route through American-controlled ground to Prague.

Upon completing their assignment in Prague, the group
obtained phony passes to motor to Berlin through Com-
munist-occupied areas.

"We didn't want to go all the way back through Ameri-
can- and English-held territory, which would mean an

extra five hundred miles," says Calvert. "So, we obtained false passes and started out."

The four Americans encountered a roadblock just outside Prague, but the sentries did not bother to flag them down. Along the way to Berlin, they stopped off in Dresden and viewed the city in which almost a quarter of a million people were killed in a massive air attack.

They reached the Autobahn at Dresden and drove straight for Berlin. "We finally pulled into Berlin at night in a pouring rain," Calvert continues. "Moe interrogated more scientists there. We had by now a clear idea of what the Russians were up to. We found out they were picking up bodies first, then whole families. They were kidnapping scientists and their families."

Orders had come from Stalin to round up some five thousand German scientists. Trucks with red stars on their doors queued up in streets in Communist Berlin as armed Russian soldiers went from house to house ordering astonished scientists and their families to board the vehicles outside. A long trip to remote parts of Russia awaited the majority of them. They were told they were to work for Russia for five years before being allowed to return to Germany. German equipment also was hauled to Russia, since the Russians had little of their own.

Bachelor scientists were provided women. A few of the celebrated scientists received generous treatment, including villas on the Black Sea. Stalin used any means to exploit their talents.

Berg learned that Russia had corralled trainloads of rocket scientists. Some of them had been assistants to Wehrner von Braun. Stalin's aim for the future was clear

Moe Berg in the Swiss Alps, February 1946.

— he would base his international power on rocketry.

While Russia engaged in these wholesale roundups, official United States policy limited the number of German scientists coming to its shores. This policy was largely shaped by the American public, which opposed importing persons from former enemy countries, particularly scientists.

The irony was that most of the German scientists preferred working in the United States to the Soviet Union. Moe Berg was approached by scores of German scientists expressing a desire to come to America. Before he recommended any of them for work in his country, Moe put them through rigid screening. He thoroughly checked out their reliability and political background. He summarily rejected any pro-Nazi scientists. Moe was unforgiving of the crimes committed by the Nazi regime, but he found American policy severe, and detrimental to its future in science. There were hundreds of qualified anti-Nazi German scientists overlooked in the selection process.

"We probably made a mistake," Calvert says, referring to American policy. "As far as our targets were concerned, we had the big ones. We had all the uranium. We had our job done. I'm not one to judge on whether or not we should have gone in and got the second layer of scientists or the third layer; the young ones. That's probably what we should have done. The Russians went in and got the young brains while we had already gotten the older ones."

Stalin's ambitious program soon realized amazing results. With the help of German scientists, Russia launched its first rocket on October 30, 1947. This event was followed by more spectacular feats, culminating in the blastoff of *Sputnik I*, an achievement that jolted an apathetic America. Before the United States was able to catch Russia in the space race, a massive effort, involving the expenditure of billions of dollars, had to be undertaken.

Berg expressed bitter disappointment over Russia's success in the hunt for the German scientists. "He told me," recalls Edward Sanger, a close friend of Berg's, "that he was very upset over it. Moe always felt we had made a great mistake in not bringing more German scientists to America."

In January 1946, General Groves ordered Berg to Copenhagen to investigate the activities of a Russian scientist reportedly spotted leaving the residence of Niels Bohr. Bohr had come to the United States in 1943 and served in an advanced capacity at the Los Alamos laboratories, where the atomic bombs were constructed. He had been awarded the Nobel Prize for physics in 1922. His research into atomic structure led to the Bohr theory of the atom, which describes the atom as a dynamic system of electrons rotating about a nucleus. Bohr had returned to Copenhagen in 1945 and become involved in the peaceful uses of atomic energy.

Groves was concerned about the kind of information the Russian scientist had obtained. The Manhattan Project leader had no idea at that time that Russia already knew America's atomic bomb secrets, which had been given to Russia by the German-born English scientist Klaus Fuchs. The son of a minister, Fuchs was assigned to the Los Alamos mission, where he had a front-row seat at the bomb's construction.

A secret U.S. government report reveals that Berg spent

two days in Copenhagen. The report states that during his interview with Bohr, Moe was informed that the only item the Dane gave the Russian "was a partial set of the *U.S. Journal of Physics.*" Berg cabled Groves that the Russian had gained nothing from his visit with Bohr.

The government document states: "General Groves was very thankful for the information from Berg and the speed with which it was obtained and reported."

10
Later Years

WHILE MOE BERG CONTINUED to handle vital postwar assignments in Europe, the OSS dissolved amid controversy. The events leading to the agency's demise resulted from a proposal by William Donovan, who sought a permanent OSS intelligence structure. Donovan had submitted a plan to President Roosevelt in 1944 seeking the creation of such a structure. The memorandum was leaked to the press, inciting editorials and generating fear that an American-style Gestapo might be born.

Before he could decide on the controversial proposal, Roosevelt died in April 1945, and the plan's fate was left for President Truman's consideration. Truman issued an executive order September 20, 1945, disbanding OSS. The dismembered spy organization was dispersed among various government departments. Secret Intelligence, to which Berg belonged, was transferred to the War Department's Strategic Services Unit.

Disenchantment followed the breakup. Many of Berg's

friends resigned. Finally, Berg, too, decided to leave because, according to reports, he felt he wasn't being used properly. His resignation became effective October 19, 1946. His departure was quiet and received no publicity.

Moe returned to Newark to live with his brother. While there he was notified he had been recommended for the Medal of Merit, the highest honor given to civilians during wartime. In recommending the medal for Berg, Lieutenant Colonal Dix cited Moe's major accomplishments in keeping General Groves informed of the German atomic bomb efforts, and other missions. The recommendation said that Lieutenant Colonel Calvert complimented Berg for his role in the critical roundup of the scientists.

The ten-page letter of recommendation for the award, sent to Colonel William Quinn of the Strategic Service Unit, reads, in part:

Dear Colonel Quinn:

This letter is written to you in the manner requested by you at my meeting with you and Colonel Pruden. The letter refers to the possibility of award of the Medal for Merit for Morris Berg. . . .

You indicated that the information which we felt should be used to support the recommendation of Medal for Merit would be a memorandum to you and would be kept in the SSU files and not go beyond the organization, and would not be made part of the wording of the Commendation.

In that light, I should like to make some definite comments as I knew them when in OSS and directly handling the United States end of the work. The comments are regarding circumstances and procedures by Mr. Berg . . . ones which turned out to be exceptionally helpful in the conduct of the war, and especially in the conduct of the procedures in General Groves' office and at the plants manufacturing the bombs. . . .

I would like first to comment upon Mr. Berg's work in Italy. He was originally set up with a submarine for the procurement of the two best Italian scientists on the atomic bomb topic. Many of the arrangements had been made. The capitulation of Italy eliminated the use of the submarine and allowed Mr. Berg to enter Rome two days after it fell and to talk with both of these Italian scientists, and with several of the other scientists who were particularly versed in nuclear physics. . . .

Among the other Italian scientists whom Mr. Berg interviewed was Dr. Antonio Ferri (former Major in the Italian Army). Dr. Ferri was the best qualified aeronautical engineer in Italy and was head of Guidonia High Speed Wind Tunnel. . . .

I am sure that Dr. Hunsacker of National Advisory Committee on Aeronautics will be very glad to give a summary of the great advantages to the U.S. Government of having Dr. Ferri available and used at Langley Field. As you know, Dr. Ferri saved this Government at least two years in very important development work. . . .

From Italy Mr. Berg proceeded to London, Paris and Bern. The information through Mr. Berg's efforts in Switzerland is documented in OSS cables received between May 1944, and May 1945, and there are many instances in which he risked his life to obtain some exceptional information.

About this information, General Groves indicated that had it not been for the information on the status of the German scientists on this work that General Groves would have overworked several of his scientists and that they would have passed away before the first U.S. bomb was completed. He said that the guidance obtained through work in Switzerland and France permitted him to gauge the pressure placed upon his scientists and he was thereby able to gauge the ability of the United States to produce two usable bombs before the war was over without "killing off" his own scientists.

Supporting the above comments and setting forth other information which is interesting and valuable in regard to the general request of this letter, I would like to indicate as follows:

That in January, 1944, we learned that there were nearly 700 tons of Belgium Congo Uranium ore in Belgium and this was sent to Duisburg, Germany, by the Germans. Later 42 tons were returned to a Belgium factory for the production of ammonium uranite. In August, 1945, Mr. Berg reported after his return to the United States that this ore was in barrels at Neustadt-Glewe near Weismar, Germany, and that he had procured pictures of the barrels and markings, and that he was working on arrangements to follow the barrels to their destination.

On December 18, 1944, Mr. Berg sat in a lecture given by Heisenberg, the manager of the atomic work in Germany and considered by many to be the best German on the atomic bomb subject. This lecture was on theoretical physics and on the status of some of the then work in Germany. . . . There were twenty people present, including several pro-Nazi scientists. Mr. Berg's ability to understand several languages permitted him to follow the lecture and afterwards discuss points with some of them. Reports on this meeting were forwarded immediately. . . . At this meeting much information was obtained by Mr. Berg on the then present status of the German and French developments. Joliot in France, and a leaner toward Nazism, was also working on this topic and the Germans had provided Joliot with much information and apparatus. . . .

Approximately December 31, 1944, Mr. Berg learned the Germans felt that successful developments would require two years. Also he learned that a supercyclotron was being built at Bisingen. This development included preparations for work on thorium.

. . . about the middle of February [1945], Mr. Berg learned that I. G. Farben was backing the cyclotron installation at Bisingen and that there had been some discussion among the German scientists as to the scope of work to be done at the cyclotron and that one of the main German scientists was overruled by the others and that the result was substantially negative. . . .

By reason of Mr. Berg's pinpointing the locations of the German scientists on the atom bomb topic, Heisenberg, von Weiszacker, von Laue, Hahn, Diebner and the others were taken directly after V-E Day [to Farm Hall, England]. . . . General Groves' European representative, Lieutenant Colonel Calvert, working out of the U.S. Embassy in London, complimented OSS and Mr. Berg on the pinpointing of the main scientists in the Heichengen-Bisingen areas.

It was learned that Hitler made it very uncomfortable for several months prior to April 1945 for Heisenberg, who was managing the German bomb developments, and at times Heisenberg did not give to Hitler all of the information developed.

After V-E Day information regarding the bomb topic and special people in France, Austria, Czechoslovakia and in the Russian controlled area of Berlin, was quickly and thoroughly learned and checked by Lieutenant Colonel Calvert and Mr. Berg taking a trip through those countries. Colonel Calvert from General Groves' office did not speak the languages but Mr. Berg did and he pinpointed many of the persons he knew of and Lieutenant Colonal Calvert took down the information and forwarded it directly to General Groves. . . .

Referring again to Mr. Berg's work for National Advisory Committee on Aeronautics and beside obtaining Major Ferri, as noted above, for NACA, it was recently stated to the writer by John Stack, chief of high speed experimental work at Langley Field of NACA, that Mr. Berg's trip to Goettingin to carry out investigations with Dr. Robinson of NACA was most helpful. That trip produced the collection of approximately 80% of the information of the German development work on high speed aeronautical designs and tests. Dr. Hunsacker, director, and Dr. Robinson, engineer of NACA, can corroborate this assistance at any time. Again, language ability and educational background and knowledge of U.S. and European educators and ability to ask direct questions and discuss subjects, as Mr. Berg has done heretofore, was of immeasurable assistance to NACA in obtaining quickly the most desirable information.

Regarding the bacteriological warfare work in which Mr. Berg was also involved, it is believed that Colonel Skinner of SSU can give the high points of Mr. Berg's work in Europe. Mr. Berg was briefed on this subject and was given the main "indicators" for him and any of his representatives to work with. It was learned in Switzerland and in France that the Germans did not have an active, large scale skilled operation on this subject.

It is, in view of the above accomplishments and the several times of risking his life, that the writer wishes to again recommend that Mr. Berg be given the Medal for Merit.

The medal was awarded Berg but he refused it, writing to Quinn on December 12, 1946:

Dear Colonel Quinn:

I have your letter of 6 December. On 2 December, on being notified of the award, I wrote your Colonel Skinner: "I regret that I must refuse to accept and I reject the medal awarded me. I do this with due respect for the spirit with which it is offered." I am grateful to those War Department officials who were kind enough, under the circumstances, to offer this award for my very modest contribution. But I cannot accept it.

Moe never related to anyone why he refused the award, but friends registered no surprise when they were told, saying it was typical of Moe to turn it down.

With the life of a spy behind him, Moe Berg attempted to adjust to being a civilian once again. It wasn't easy.

"I sensed a radical change in Moe's behavior soon after he had come home from Europe," Samuel Berg recalls. "He was not the same affable Moe that I knew. His behavior was strange. He had become snappish on occasion. That was not like Moe. I think the major reason for this change was his wartime work.

"Moe never told me about his missions, but, when he showed me the vial of potassium cyanide he had to carry with him, I knew he had been in tough and dangerous spots. I really admired him when I learned of the cyanide. He also carried pistols with him that he showed me. The cyanide and pistols were so foreign to him — to the Moe that I knew.

"He was a man who became distressed at the sight of blood. He could not stomach it. Nor could he see people sick; he could not stand sickness. Moe's missions obviously had a tremendous impact on him."

Compounding his wartime experiences was a business failure that left Moe humiliated and bitter. In the early 1930s, he had become a partner in a stationery business with a four-thousand-dollar investment. The company grew rapidly and Moe's original investment multiplied. During the war, his profits — estimated to have been close to a quarter of a million dollars — were pumped back into his business. But the firm, and his profits, evaporated after Moe's business partner decided to expand.

"It was as though Moe was broke for all it ever mattered," Dr. Berg recalls. "He never saw any of the money."

The firm's expansion was predicated on a government contract that was never signed.

"The government kept after us for more of the kind of

tape we were manufacturing," the partner said. "They offered us a five-million-dollar contract. I knew it was risky to expand without a signed contract. We were doing well, but agreeing to the government offer meant finding a bigger building to work in and buying costly equipment. The government insisted it needed our material. I felt it was my patriotic duty to immediately go ahead with the expansion and sign the contract later.

"We rented a building on Long Island for forty thousand dollars a year and invested heavily in new equipment. In several months, the war was over and the government stopped its orders. They weren't obligated to do business with us. The contract hadn't been signed. Suddenly, our business was in deep trouble."

Berg was crushed, not because of his own loss, but because five hundred people employed by the firm now faced the grim prospect of losing their jobs.

"Money meant nothing to Moe," his partner said. "He was an unselfish man. He was more concerned about the workers and the creditors we owed money to. He came to me and said, 'How much do you need to keep the business going?' I said, 'Two hundred thousand dollars.' He said, 'You've got it.'

"He went to Chicago to visit a rich friend for a loan. When he came back two weeks later, I never saw him so depressed in my life. He had been rejected by a friend. You see, friends were the most important thing in Moe's life. Moe said to me, 'He was a friend,' and couldn't understand why he was refused."

That money had little value for Moe was illustrated at a New York City meeting with Lawrence Houston, an OSS officer who is now chief counsel of the CIA, held after the war as a result of Berg's resistance to completing an accounting of his expenses as a secret agent. Moe possessed an almost pathological distaste for filling out forms.

Government records show Berg earned a little more than sixteen thousand dollars for the three years he was in OSS. He also had carried huge sums of money to pay for information. When the government persisted for an accounting of his expenses, Berg became so upset he volunteered to reimburse the government his sixteen-thousand-dollar salary.

The government, however, went ahead and reconstructed Berg's expenses, determining that he was owed three thousand dollars.

Houston states: "I met with Berg in New York to ask him how he wished this sum to be handled. He flatly refused to accept it, and in spite of my arguments he was adamant, although extremely pleasant and polite." Houston adds he was at a loss to "explain the basis for his refusal."

After Moe failed to raise the money in Chicago, there was little that he could do to prevent the firm from going bankrupt. Creditors demanded to be paid. Moe borrowed from friends — a few thousand dollars here and there — to pay off some of the debts.

J. Russell Forgan, Wall Street banker, said of Moe's effort: "It was one of the finest things in the man's life. He told me, 'I'm going to pay off all the debts. I'm going to make them good.' Legally, he did not have to."

The stationery firm finally went under, but that was not the end of Moe's worries. The IRS charged that he had neglected payment of income taxes over a period of three years during the war and figured Moe owed the government between sixty and eighty thousand dollars in taxes. Although the profits had been pumped back into the business, they were taxable, the government said.

Dr. Berg says: "Moe was not making the kind of money in OSS needed to pay the taxes, so he told the IRS, 'I can't pay that.' The IRS began calling the shots, saying, 'You are committed by law to pay this to the government.' And, I think, that is when Moe decided he would not earn more than enough money needed to get by. That is, he would not take a job paying over a certain level because the extra would have to go to IRS. I think that was the turning point in Moe's life."

Moe's reaction to these setbacks was to plunge into the serenity of study. He devoured books on language, philosophy, astronomy and atomic energy. For weeks on end he lived a hermitlike existence with his books that grew tall in stack after stack in his brother's home. Moe laid down his books for visits with closely selected friends, scientific conferences, and ball games. In 1947, he was reunited in New York with Edwin Hubble, world-famous astronomer whom he had met in his early OSS days. Hubble had come east for a weekend of conferences. After they had lunch together, Hubble called on a friend of his, Anita Loos, author of *Gentlemen Prefer Blondes*.

Miss Loos recalls:

"Edwin Hubble and his wife, Grace, were friends of mine while I was in Hollywood. Edwin was head of the Mount Wilson Observatory at Cal Tech and was one of our greatest astronomers. He called me when he was in

New York for a weekend after the war and said, 'I'm going to give you the greatest experience you've probably ever known. I'm going to bring Moe Berg to your apartment. I want you to meet him.'

"Well, they came. And Edwin, in introducing Moe, said, 'God only knows how many lives he saved during the war.' Moe brushed that off. Well, Edwin was right. Moe was the most intriguing conversationalist and certainly most extraordinary man I have ever met. Moe was in the Clark Gable mold. Terribly handsome, with terrific manners. A real Old World gentleman. I was a great friend of Aldous Huxley, who spoke sixteen languages. But that was, you know, a matter of culture. Moe put his languages to work.

"I admired Moe because he sought no publicity. He retreated to his private interests. No one ever knew where Moe was. I would call his brother upon occasion and the doctor wasn't sure where Moe had gone. I remember writing to him once at a hotel in Boston, but the letter was returned."

Arthur Daley experienced the same difficulty in finding the catcher. "He was the one reliable man you would see at each World Series, but generally it was difficult to find Moe after the war," he explains. "Once I went to the Polo Grounds, and around the seventh inning I saw this lone figure sitting in the right-field stands. It looked like Moe. I went there and it was Moe. He had a newspaper in his hands and appeared very serious. I'm not sure what he had read or what influenced the comment, but he said, I remember, 'Arthur, Arthur, the awful thing in this world, like that game down there, is in the late innings, and there isn't any room for an error.'

"We had a nice chat that friends do. I said, 'Moe, you're a valuable man to keep in contact with, but I don't know your phone number.' Moe said, 'Write this down, Arthur.' He gave me his brother's number."

Rumors of Berg's espionage exploits began mounting. In a column in the *Boston Herald American*, writer Bob Considine, longtime Berg friend, said of the catcher, "I always thought that he was assigned to outrageously dangerous OSS work in Germany to kill, as quietly as possible, German physicists working on Hitler's atomic bomb." Considine said he asked Moe if this were true, but the athlete would not comment. Adds Samuel Berg, "Moe was loathe to talk about his activities. Just to illustrate his disinclination towards divulging any information, in 1949 I gave a lecture at the Newark Museum on the effects of the atomic bomb. The talk was open to the public. Moe and several of our mutual friends attended. I mentioned that Nagasaki was not the first choice for the second bomb, that Kokura was the primary target. I said Kokura was clouded in and, so Nagasaki was selected.

"Moe turned to our friends and said, 'I wished he wouldn't have said that. He never should have divulged that secret.' Of course, this was no longer a secret. It already had appeared in newspapers, but it showed how adamant he was in maintaining secrecy which he vowed. He maintained that even towards me."

Norman Newhouse, an executive with Newhouse newspapers and a former OSS officer, said, "It wasn't until years after the war that I knew how important a role Moe Berg played for OSS."

The reason Moe would not relate his activities, includ-

ing to interested biographers, was that many persons in
Europe, mainly those in the scientific community sympathetic to the Allied cause, had to be protected through
silence, at least in the early postwar period; Moe's atomic
spying remained top secret. Moreover, General Groves,
who assessed Moe in his memoirs as a "very reliable and
able OSS agent," was equally adamant against publicizing
Berg's critical atomic role. Lieutenant Colonel Calvert recalls meeting Groves in New York City. "We discussed
Moe," Calvert said, "but I got the impression Groves had a
'hold' on releasing any information about him." The
Manhattan Project chief would only generalize about
Moe's role. He told *Newark Evening News* writer Guy
Savino: "Moe Berg was of tremendous importance to us
because he could talk so many languages with such fluency.
There was more to his knowledge than mere conversa-
tional ability. He had the athlete's poise and the courage of
an intelligent man who was supremely confident in his
own ability."

The world of science continued to fascinate Berg. He
kept abreast of the latest discoveries and developments by
maintaining regular contacts with scientists and attending
meetings of the American Physical Society, a leading scientific organization.

Dr. William Fowler, head of the Kellogg Radiation
Laboratory at Cal Tech, recalls being introduced to Moe
in 1947 at the home of Professor Howard P. Robertson.

"Thereafter," Fowler relates, "I met Moe on the average
about once a year. He would show up out of nowhere at
meetings of the American Physical Society in New York or
Washington, and would go along with me to sessions I was

interested in. Eventually we would find a quiet place to talk and reminisce for an hour or so, or have lunch together, and then Moe would disappear just as mysteriously as he had arrived.

"Moe was interested in physics, mathematics and astronomy and understood enough to enjoy conversations and discussions between professionals. He especially enjoyed the sometimes vehement arguments small groups would get into at Physical Society meetings in the hallways. In fact, I recall that several times in such discussions I would turn around and there would be Moe, who clearly had come up from behind to eavesdrop.

"Moe was closemouthed about his wartime experiences, but he did tell me one part of his mission involving an Italian scientist. As Moe told the story, he won over the suspicious Italian by quoting Petrarch.

"I admired Moe as a man primarily because he was that rare combination — an athlete and an intellectual. He was an intelligent, sensitive man. He was entertaining and he was clever. Clearly, he lived by his wits."

Berg's cultural breadth surprised unsuspecting scientists who had heard of him as a professional baseball player. Dr. John H. Van Vleck, professor emeritus of Harvard University's physics department, first met Moe at a meeting of the American Philosophical Society in Philadelphia. "Somehow or other my wife, Abigail, ended up next to Moe at the dinner," Van Vleck remembers. "I wondered what she could possibly find to discuss with Moe since she is not a baseball fan, but they obviously were having an interesting and vivacious conversation. Straining my ears a little I discovered that they were discussing the relics of the Egyptian tombs in the museum at Cairo."

Moe maintained close ties with many foreign scientists he had met in Europe who were now living in the United States. He always expressed concern over their adjustment to life in America.

One of these scientists was accused of harboring Communist sympathies during Senator Joseph McCarthy's witch-hunts in the early 1950s. The man held a teaching post at Columbia University at the time and was threatened with deportation. When Moe learned of his friend's difficulties he was disturbed.

"Moe was instrumental in bringing this scientist to America," Ted Sanger, friend of Berg and a Princeton alumnus, says. "Moe felt this man represented anything but a threat to the country. In fact, he felt the scientist was a fantastic asset. Moe took the position that, if the scientist was going to be put on the boat, he [Moe] was going to leave the country on the same boat."

Writing of the incident in the *Trentonian* (a Trenton, New Jersey, Daily) years later, Jay Dunn, a friend, said Moe felt that threatening to deport himself "was the only way to save the neck of the educator, who had been highly co-operative with American intelligence during the war. It also forced the hand of the University president, Dwight David Eisenhower, who had tried to avoid involvement."

Subsequently, the scientist was cleared of McCarthy's charges and remained in the United States. The episode had a lasting impact on Moe's views of Eisenhower. In the two presidential contests between Eisenhower and Adlai Stevenson, Moe was to become a strong booster of the Democrat.

"Moe admired Adlai Stevenson," Sanger recalls. "He

admired his liberality, his mind, and his work. Certainly
nobody has spoken the English language with greater facility in modern times than he, and Moe appreciated this. I
think Moe felt it was a tragedy for the country that Stevenson never got to be President."

Moe had been friendly at Princeton with the two-time
Democratic presidential candidate, who had graduated
from Princeton in 1922. "Moe knew Stevenson very well,"
remembers S. Lang Makrauer, Berg's college classmate.
"When Princeton dedicated the bronze bust of Stevenson
in the Woodrow Wilson School, Moe was there. This was
strictly a by-invitation-only affair."

In 1951, Berg was asked by the government to come to
Washington to discuss scientific subjects, particularly reports leaking out of Russia of the dramatic advances being
achieved behind the Iron Curtain. Berg buried the bitter-
ness that still engulfed him over the IRS matter, which he
was to settle in three years for a reported five thousand
dollars, and went to the capital. During a subrosa meeting,
Moe was informed of the Russian situation and asked to
reenter government service. He agreed.

According to Lawrence Houston of the CIA, Moe's assignment was to "advise and consult on foreign scientific
programs, particularly concerning Soviet and satellite science." Berg was "never a staff employee of CIA, but had a
contractual relationship with the agency." Moe spent five
months conferring with scientists in Europe. His probing
confirmed to the government that Russian science was indeed on the threshold of historic achievements in space.

After his assignment, Moe visited Mike Burke, who was
then living in Bad Homburg, Germany. "Moe came for a

few days' visit and stayed four months," Burke remembers. "My house was virtually turned into a publishing plant. He covered the place with every newspaper he could find, and left notes to the maid warning, 'Don't disturb — they're alive!' "

Moe Berg's association with the government was interrupted for five years when he returned to the United States, where his reason for living seemed to be constant study. But, after Russia launched *Sputnik I* in 1957, he agreed to assume a vital role in the North Atlantic Treaty Organization's defense structure. He joined the staff of Theodore von Karman, head of NATO's Advisory Group for Aeronautical Research and Development (AGARD). Von Karman, considered the world's greatest aeronautical scientist, before his death in 1963, conceived AGARD to "insure NATO countries that they would always have the best technology at their command." Moe had met von Karman through Antonio Ferri. The catcher's priority with AGARD involved working with scientists and military personnel of other nations in determining where NATO's missile-launching base should be centered. Three countries were being considered for the base: Portugal, Italy, and Turkey.

Despite his short tenure with AGARD, a warm relationship developed between Moe and von Karman. When von Karman received America's first National Medal of Science from President John F. Kennedy in February 1963, Moe was among the invited guests. During the ceremonies, President Kennedy approached Moe and shook his hand. "Moe," the President said, "baseball hasn't been the same without you." Moe replied, "Thank you, Mr. President. I'd like to think that that was true."

Moe left von Karman's group, but friends believed he was still in government service. Samuel Goudsmit lends credence to that belief: "There was one incident that worried me and still does. It was in late 1958 or so. I met Moe in New York and we went to the Museum of Modern Art. We had lunch there. I had a little envelope with some paper in it. After I'd gone through the lunch .line the envelope was gone. Someone had taken it. It was of no value at all. But someone must have said, 'There's Berg and Goudsmit together. Something must be up.' "

Only limited evidence suggests that Moe had any connection with the government after 1960. Goudsmit recalls: "Moe was a valued friend, but then he dropped out of sight. I tried to find him through his brother and friends, but they did not know where he was. I even asked the FBI where he was. The FBI knew. They told me, 'Don't worry. He's all right.' But they would not say where he was.

"I knew he bought several newspapers daily and one day I planted a cryptogram in the Sunday *New York Herald Tribune*. The cryptogram read, 'Moe Berg, where are you?' I had hoped he would react. He never did."

Many of Moe's new friends were not aware of what he was doing for a livelihood. Hugh and Mary Townley, for example, were artists living in Boston when they met Moe. Mary Townley recalls: "We met him in the late fifties and saw a great deal of him over the next few years. As far as I could tell he did not have a job obligating him to be anywhere at a particular time."

Hugh Townley, then an art teacher at Boston University and now at Brown University, said, "I was convinced at that time, and I still am, that he was working for somebody in government. He was far too mobile and was always traveling.

"He was a totally surprising man; you could see him in a restaurant in Cambridge at lunch and then run into him by accident in a Boston restaurant that night.

"There was this nervous vitality about him; a great animal content which had to do with awareness. He possessed an intelligence which was not usual. He also had the rest of these human qualities which you think are endearing.

"A favorite Boston restaurant of Moe's was Jake Wirth's. I remember having lunch with him there one afternoon and receiving one of forty language lessons from him. In this case it was a sign in Latin over the bar. He translated it into English for me: 'To each his own taste.' "

The Townleys had been introduced to Moe by Ted Sanger, who had met Berg in Boston during the Boston Braves–Cleveland Indians World Series in 1948. Sanger, director of the Shaw Prep School on Boylston Street, said, "Occasionally, Moe could be persuaded to come to the school and lecture. He would talk about language or baseball or whatever from his broad world of knowledge. The students found him fascinating, but it was the perceptive student that particularly found this so.

"Moe never really looked upon his work as a job. I think he felt that what he was doing was taking one assignment or case at a time and being free from other constraints. His object in doing it was the job, and to do it well, and not the money that might or might not result from it. I know that a good number of his jobs didn't result in any payments. He helped people selflessly."

Jay Dunn was in his twenties, writing for the *Trentonian* sports pages when he met Moe:

"I remember one game I was covering at Shea Stadium between the Mets and the Braves. Phil Niekro, the knuckleballer, was pitching for Atlanta. His catcher was Bob Didier. There were runners on base all day for the Mets. After the game, and before I started for the clubhouse, Moe asked me what player I was going to talk to. I really hadn't made up my mind. He suggested that I interview the Braves catcher and ask him how he ever handled Niekro's knuckleball. I did, and Didier's comments were real interesting. I wrote a column on the catcher's remarks concerning the difficulties of handling a knuckle-ball pitcher.

"Another aspect of his personality which amazed me was his refusal ever to be bullied, or see anyone else bullied, on a major point. He had an equal dislike for any sort of small squabble. During a Princeton-Rutgers foorball game (I happen to be a Rutgers alumnus) he sat down next to me in the press box and said, 'In your honor, I'm going to root for Rutgers today.' The notion of two people seated side by side rooting for different teams bothered him."

Berg often visited *Boston Globe* sports columnist Arthur Siegel, whose book-filled apartment was a haven for Boston newspapermen who shared Siegel's insomnia.

Siegel once asked: "Moe, do I detect second thoughts in you. Was that damn ball game and all the mystery stuff worth it. Wasn't Mr. Chips a better bet?"

"Arthur," replied Berg, "I seek no other man's shoes. If I've misdirected my priorities, and I'm confident that this is not so, I've had a pretty fair time in lost country. There are no regrets. I loved every day on the ball field and the gentlemen who played it in my time. Even grandmothers should experience the pure excitement of covering home plate with an ape charging home, cleats flying high.

"As for old Chips, Arthur, he was a lovely guy. But I always suspected Chips dashed madly about campus trying to find his way off of it. But those winding campus sidewalks confused the poor man.

"And if I'm on the boulevard of second thoughts, I made a wrong turn somewhere. Tomorrow I'm going to breakfast with a red robin and, if the gods are charitable, there'll be a chickadee along."

Siegel replied, "Moe, I know a few grandmothers who I'd love to see behind the plate at Fenway Park, cleats high and retaliatory, charging home."

Siegel's three guests, glasses raised high, toasted grandmothers worthy of catching duty.

"Moe you said nothing, rather obviously so, of the mystery business. You were never any mystery to me. You just couldn't hit too well and didn't want the pitchers to look bad. But, seriously, Moe, the rumors over the years suggest some extraordinary moments in the life of a third-string catcher. Besides, this guy needs a column. What do you say?"

"Arthur, friend," replied Berg, "I've generally loved you fourth estate-people. That maiden's curiosity never abandons your collective makeup. And that's really wonderful, wonderful. I consider whatever I may have done nothing extraordinary, and were I not a ballplayer there would have been no talk at all. The little man, who has always been the great man, pays for his anonymity, I'm afraid."

Siegel shook his head as the others broke into soft laughter. Obviously, there would be no discussion of Moe's still secret wartime exploits. Instead, the subject turned to which team Moe considered his favorite.

"Boston was kind to me. I loved the city," he said. "Yawkey and Cronin were gentlemen and my crowd in that bullpen made life marvelous, marvelous. Bobby Doerr, Teddy, Wilson, Pytlak, Auker, Cascarella, Schacht. Wonderful, wonderful.

"But Chicago provided the real test of my ability and I would like to think that I passed. The years with the White Sox were my favorite."

Months passed into years. Moe displayed no change in his life pattern. It was not uncommon now to see him on his way to a bookstore with the only concession ever to his nocturnal wardrobe — a black umbrella to assist his stride. He appeared a Chamberlain without Czechoslovakia.

The aura surrounding him remained undimmed among newspapermen and his carefully chosen friends. Tommy Thomas recalls Moe's visit to his home in Pennsylvania Dutch country. "He came down to see us wearing his traditional black suit, black tie, black everything. He had only a toothbrush and a razor blade. Moe came during a drought. It hadn't rained in months. And, God, he took his standard three baths a day!

"Moe was the cleanest man in the world. He took a bath at eight-thirty in the morning, four-thirty in the afternoon, and eleven-thirty at night. He bathed for an hour at a time. We ran out of towels in the house and, worse, we ran out of water. My wife, Alice, was fascinated by him. We'd sit on the porch and Moe would point out the galaxies and constellations. The dippers, Ursa Minor, Ursa Major, Orion, the Milky Way. Stars captivated him. We'd have friendly little arguments and Moe would use the idiom of Dutch country, saying, 'Now, Tommy, listen to me out. Listen to me out.'

"One of the real joys Moe got was discussing his friend, Matsumoto. Moe had heard that Matsumoto had helped American POWs during the war. Moe was very proud of that." Matsumoto served in the Japanese diet and was vice-cabinet secretary after the war.

Crossan Cooper, the second baseman on Princeton's '23 ball club, remembers Moe's visit to Baltimore: "One day he called me and said he was in town. I said to come on over and have dinner and spend the night with us. He came, had dinner, spent the night and stayed for six weeks. He was always good company. He knew about almost anything. Moe was a very cultivated gentleman. He would never talk about his OSS exploits. I'd try to get him to talk about them, but he wouldn't."

Asa Bushnell, former commissioner of the Eastern Collegiate Athletic Conference, recalls: "Moe came to Princeton frequently to work in the library here or watch football games. I saw him a lot during the last couple of years. At that time I was suffering from what is known as the 'retirement syndrome.' I felt down. Moe would tell me, 'Asa, it's impossible for you to feel this way.' He'd make special trips down here to see me. He always left me feeling good."

Moe worked little during the last seven years of his life. An occasional law case provided pocket money. Having played baseball in the days prior to the players' pension, he received no retirement money from the sport which devoured his good years. And there was no government pension.

He never let anyone know of his worsening financial plight, nor did he seek reentry into baseball when he returned from Europe. Tom Yawkey maintains:

"Moe could have come to the Red Sox anytime. He loved the game, but he never expressed a desire to me to come back, and, as far as I ever heard, not to anyone else. Without question, he could have gotten a job with us. He might have fit better in the front office. In my book there's always room for intelligence in any organization.

"If he had ever told me he wanted to come back, I certainly would have been very happy to find him a place that would have been agreeable with him."

And Ted Lyons adds, "Moe was so full of pride, foolish pride. He just couldn't change."

Moe Berg's pursuit of knowledge intensified as his face confronted age and his once coal-black hair grayed above great, black eyebrows. Books and newspapers, once his obsession, were now his masters. They allowed him little else in life.

In 1965 a book crisis of unimaginable proportions developed in the Berg home. As Samuel Berg relates it:

"Moe filled every available space in my house with his books and newspapers. There was a virtual confrontation between his massive book collection and my medical books. And my books were being overwhelmed. The place was overrun with literature. It was difficult to navigate. You had to move sideways. Having guests at the house was out of the question. They would have had to sit on books stacked high on every chair. I don't know how Moe slept, but it had to be in between books which covered his bed.

"To compound the situation, Moe had a bad habit of underlining everything he read that he thought was important, with a soft lead pencil. He thought everything was important. The only words he failed to underline were 'the,' 'and,' and 'or.'

"If you looked at a book he had read, the whole damn thing was marked in black. It was very unpleasant trying to read a book he had read.

"Further, after arriving home each night, the first thing Moe would do is take a shower, don a Japanese kimono, come down to the library, where he often spent the entire night reading, underlining passages. Often he would leave the library in his kimono, his head buried in a book and walk past some of my patients, who couldn't believe their eyes. Moe would have been right at home in a Roman toga.

"These books and magazines and papers that filled up my house were a source of conflict between us. Moe moved a few blocks away. I asked him to do that. It was the only way to resolve the problem. Moe had thousands of books. We put the books in one hundred huge cartons and loaded them onto a truck. The truck had to make three trips to move the books alone. It took another truckload to move the newspapers he had collected."

Studying hundreds of Berg's books, underlined pencil marks, and marginal notes gave researchers a feeling of moving through a coal mine.

Berg bought *Caesar and Pompey* in Greece, a school classic edition published by Ginn in 1900, and Moe's pencil found it important to underline that Caesar, aside from the obvious known about him, had in 68 B.C. held the office of quaestor and in 65 B.C. that of aedile. Further, it was important to Berg that "on motion of the tribune Vatinius, it was voted by the people that after his consulship, Caesar should receive Gallia, Cisalpina and Illyricum as his province and that he should have three legions."

In a second-edition Russian grammar book, by Dr. Nevill Forbes of Oxford University, published by Oxford Press, Berg underlined hundreds of lines relating to Russians, the history of their alphabet, and grammar. Concerning the alphabet Berg underlined:

The alphabet used by the Russians and the other Slavs of the orthodox confession, Serbians and Bulgarians, for the rendering of their sounds of their language is that known as the Cyrillic. It is so called because its composition is attributed to St. Cyril (826–869) a Greek of Salonika, whose secular name was Constantine, who with his brother Methodius was commissioned by the Emperor Michael 2nd, to effect the conversion of Moravia, the Prince of Moravia having expressed the wish to see Christianity introduced into his country. Confronted with the problem how to communicate the truth to the savages of Pannonia, he, with great ingenuity, elaborated an alphabet which with scientific accuracy represented the sounds of the Slavonic vernacular, so different from those of Greek . . . whether it was of the alphabet now called Cyrillic that St. Cyril was the author, or of the cognate alphabet called Glagolitic, still used in remote parts of Dalmatia, is uncertain, but it is probable that of the two, the latter, the Glagolitic, which has been proved to be older than the Cyrillic and was founded on the Greek minuscule script of the Ninth Century, was that actually compiled by him, and was later, owing to the complexity of its character, almost everywhere supplanted by the alphabet now known as the Cyrillic, which, founded on the Greek Majuscule script, was much clearer than the Glagolitic . . . Besides Sanskrit, the only language which has a really scientific alphabet, in which every letter corresponds exactly and without help of accents to the sound it is intended to represent, is Serbian, where there was no historical tradition strong enough to obstruct reform. The Cyrillic alphabet is based on that of the Greek Majuscule script but contains important additional signs, the origin of which is now known, representing sounds which never existed in Greek.

Berg underlined many details in *Celebrated Spies and Famous Mysteries of the Great War*, written by George Barton and published by the Page Company of Boston in 1919.

In the book's introduction, Berg underlined a passage about the strength of femininity: "The sublime devotion of a martyr nurse and the recklessness of the Javanese dancer and the Turkish beauty will be remembered long after the war has passed into history."

Studying the history of the treason trial of Sir Roger Casement, executed by the British in August of 1916, Berg underlined hundreds of details cited in bringing about the conviction. "In the pocket of one of the coats was a railroad ticket from Berlin to Wilhelmshaven. . . . On the night of Thursday, April 20, 1916, John Hussey, a laborer, stood on the windswept shore of the Kerry coast and gazed toward the sea. Suddenly out of the darkness of the night, came the flashing of a red light. . . . It was an impressive scene when the King's Coroner, in accordance with tradi-

tion, arose to read the indictment. This declared that Sir
Roger Casement was to be tried under the Treason Act
passed in the days of Edward III."

To buttress his penchant for emphasis, Berg used the
margins of the pages for personal observations.

Berg's book collection was not confined to Newark.
Friends reported Berg library branches in New York,
Washington and Massachusetts. In Harvard, Massachu-
setts, Ted Sanger says:

"Moe left books here with me. You name it, he had it.
When he brought books to my home, he would say, 'Keep
these for me. I'll give instructions later.'

"Moe was an accumulator of books and his range of
interest was so wide that it would take cataloguing to make
some kind of comprehensive sense of them."

One of Moe's favorite Boston bookstores was the Brattle
Book Shop, owned by George Gloss, who remembers:

"Moe would enter my place, and after we'd exchange
greetings, he would often go to the elevated level of the
bookstore, which is to the rear. He would pick up book
after book, placing those which interested him on the
floor. He would be there for hours, sometimes the whole
day, and the book piles surrounding him got higher and
higher.

"They would go above his waist and you could only see
the upper part of his body. Customers would look up in
wonderment, not realizing who he was or that he was at his
life's work — gaining knowledge. Books on languages and
atomic energy particularly intrigued him, but his range of

interests exceeded any man I've ever known. He was a monument of knowledge.

"Bookseller colleagues of mine said Moe provided the same panorama in their shops. I recall once Moe was surrounded by books when a young man walked in. He was a Swedish gentleman and had just gotten a Guggenheim scholarship in preparation for compiling the first dictionary ever for some African nation. I think it was Nigeria. The young man asked for some books on linguistics.

"Moe overheard the young fellow's request and project. He then provided the young man with names of friend linguists in London and Africa.

"Two years later the man returned and asked me to convey his thanks to Moe Berg because his friends had been of tremendous assistance in the project."

Moe Berg's mornings, in his later years, involved early rising and a walk to various newsstands for newspapers. He tucked them under his arm and then walked to restaurants for smaller breakfasts than those of earlier years. He sat at tables reading for lengthy periods, sipping coffee. Restaurant owners in various areas asked him to leave. His lingering at tables upset them. Many knew little of Moe Berg other than he was a onetime ballplayer who had a penchant for reading. Moe Berg would fold his newspapers, place them under his once great throwing arm, and leave. Dr. Berg remembers: "Moe didn't last long in any one place. He was an unwelcome guest. He went from one restaurant to another."

"Moe found himself ensconced in a what-have-you-done-for-me-lately world," says Mike Burke.

Sanger adds, "My feeling was that he was more and more

up against a world he was out of sympathy with. The buck-chasing world distressed him. He adhered to certain hon-orable standards and he assumed business leaders would. But it's not been that kind of an era. It's been a pretty shoddy era."

Charlie Wagner remembers the last years of his friend. "It wasn't a happy Moe. In 1967 the Red Sox won the pennant and I was with him in Boston. He was happy then, happy for the team. Overall, however, the gaiety wasn't there. Perhaps there were flashes of happiness, but that's all. The subconscious wasn't happy. Something was missing. Moe wasn't himself.

"I'd go to New York and call Moe, asking that he join Tommy Thomas and me for breakfast. He'd say that he had already eaten, but we'd insist. When he finally arrived he'd order liver and onions and sweet rolls. He was true to his philosophy that you don't necessarily have to live by the book."

Ed Rumill recalls seeing Moe at the Cooperstown Hall of Fame game in 1967. "Moe seemed to prefer staying in the background of things. He had withdrawn, and was going through the motions. That marvelous exhilaration he generated was gone."

Despite his decline, Moe's magic continued to enthrall those who met him.

"Moe was the type of person you rarely meet," said Dr. W. Hardy Hendren, director of Pediatric Surgery at Mas-sachusetts General Hospital and professor of surgery at Harvard Medical School. "He possessed a charisma that attracted immediately. Once you locked on, you always made time available to be with him.

"I met Moe at a World Series game in Boston in 1967. I had gotten a seat in the press box from a sportswriter friend of mine. To my left was a young writer. To my right was a refined looking gentleman. It was Moe Berg. He turned to me and asked, 'What paper do you work for?' I told him I was there under totally false auspices. I told him I was a surgeon.

"He laughed. He said he was a former ballplayer, but I soon perceived he was not an ordinary catcher for the Red Sox. During the game, he predicted what the pitcher would throw next. I was impressed. Then I was a little skeptical when I learned of his background; of Princeton and Columbia and the White Sox. As all of this sort of unraveled, I said, 'This is a very interesting person.'

"After the game, I invited him to my home for dinner. As we left the ball park, everybody knew Moe. The guy selling peanuts said, 'Hello, Moe.' Another man in a Chesterfield said, 'Hello, Moe.'

"When he entered my home, he immediately began translating the Latin on a brass rubbing on the wall.

"That evening, we had several guests, doctors who were in Boston to work with me. As we were sitting in the dining room I said to Moe I was amazed to see him predict what sort of pitch was coming next. He said it comes easy for a professional ballplayer to do that.

"Then he mentioned that it was easy for professionals to make mistakes, too. He said, 'Occasionally surgeons make mistakes. For example, when a surgeon is operating for appendicitis and discovers it was Meckels diverticulum.' Well, the doctors dropped their forks. They could not believe their ears.

"After dinner, Moe talked privately to one of the doctors. The doctor told me afterwards Moe had asked what sort of surgery does Dr. Hendren do. He asked if I knew how to do an umbilical hernia. The next morning he was in my office. He had a great big hernia. I performed the operation.

"Moe came here one night and gave me a present. It was a two-hundred-and-three-year-old textbook on surgery. It was a lovely gift. The name of it is *Manuel du jeune chirugien*. It was published in Paris. Moe said, 'I happened to be browsing in a bookstore a number of years ago when I saw this book. I knew someday I would like to buy it and give it to someone.' There was a note inside. It read: 'For Dr. Hardy Hendren, friend and surgeon nonpareil, who is rewriting the "book" on surgery, with thanks and gratitude, Moe.'

"I felt Moe was still with government. He was always busy. His fluency in many languages, plus being very current on various issues, was not consistent with a former ballplayer. He was probably quietly engaged behind the scenes with the government. I felt he was working for the CIA. Every time we saw him we found out something new about Moe. We discovered another side to him."

Although considerable material had been written on the atomic bomb during the first twenty-five years after the war, the important role played by Moe Berg remained untold. That is how Moe Berg wanted it. In many ways there was no alternative. Yet, the great preponderance of his life — the baseball years, the linguistic achievements, his personality, the military aspects which did not threaten security — was worthy of revelation. Now, in his mid sixties, financially hurting, Moe Berg yielded.

A friend, writer and publisher Sayre Ross, recalls:

"I made arrangements to have Moe's life story done. He was to receive a thirty-five-thousand-dollar advance from a major publishing company. A meeting had been set up at the Algonquin Hotel. It was an immediate disaster.

"A young editor arrived late at the meeting and, after being introduced to Moe, said, 'It's a pleasure to meet you. I have loved all your pictures.'

"Everybody looked at everybody. Moe said, 'Pictures? Who do you think I am?'

"The editor said, 'Why, aren't you the Moe of the Three Stooges?'

"Moe was livid. He answered, 'Jesus Christ.'

"He kicked me under the table and we left. He said, 'Sayre, to hell with them, we'll do the damn book ourselves.' I said, 'Moe, it'll never happen. I've been asking you for a year and a half.'

"He said, 'No, no, honest, Sayre, we'll do the damn thing. Son of a bitch! Moe Berg of the Three Stooges! When you get editorial people ill equipped to do the job, I'll have no part of it.' He couldn't be placated. Obviously, there never was any book."

Berg sank deeper into the serenity of study. Mandarin excited his mind, particularly the northern dialect spoken in the Peking region. He devoured the language with uncommon scholarship. He mingled with the elders in Chinese communities in Boston and New York, probing their history, attentive to the sounds of the Orient. He began to speak the language.

He discussed Mandarin with Chinese scholars, vigorously enunciating the difficult sounds. Chinese newspapers joined French, Italian and Spanish papers under Moe Berg's arm. He began spending his limited fund on books relating to Chinese language.

Berg began frequenting Goodspeeds' in Boston, a store that sells antique books, and store manager Arnold Silverman, recalls:

"Moe would appear here from time to time. He put on a very good front, although I felt things were difficult for him. But he was very proud. The last time Moe was here, about 1971, he purchased books relating to the Chinese language, particularly works by French authors who did comparative French-Chinese language studies. I had heard of his remarkable ability with languages. Moe was holding a book in Chinese and I asked him if he would read for me.

"He agreed. He read passages from the book and didn't stumble. It was one thing to hear about the man's language propensity and another thing to observe it in action."

"I would say he was an authentic genius," Sanger remarks. "He had a thorough mind. He believed in doing things completely, whether it was an academic exercise or a job for somebody. He had a very high standard of performance. He was a pro in everything he attempted.

"Perhaps he got this from baseball, but I would myself say he got this from being a genius. He didn't speak a language so-so. He spoke it perfectly, or said he didn't know the language."

Dr. Hendron adds, "Moe was one of the best endowed

people, cerebrally, I have ever met. He had tremendous intellectual abilities. I think Moe was obviously of genius intellect. No question about it."

"I did not realize that I was living with a genius," Dr. Berg once said. "I believe now what a lot of people feel about my brother, that he was a genius in his own way. He was a true scholar in the sense of the dons of the twelfth and thirteenth centuries — those who founded Oxford and Cambridge. Their sole objective was to gain knowledge for knowledge's sake without intent to apply it. Material things were of little concern to Moe."

In 1972, Moe turned seventy. He still traveled as often as he could. Wherever he went, the routine usually was the same: ballgames, bookstores, libraries, newsstands.

Larry Rosenthal, who has operated the Milk Street, Boston, newsstand for forty-five years, remembers Moe from the time he was with the Red Sox.

"When he was playing here," Rosenthal said, "he would come and buy all sorts of out-of-town newspapers. He would clip items important to friends of his and mail them everywhere. He would leave foreign books for months at a time at the stand, and then, all at once would show up for them. I hadn't seen him for a few years and then, he appeared at the stand one day in 1972, put his arms around me, patted me on the back and said, 'Larry, wonderful to see you. Wonderful, wonderful.' "

Moe seldom looked to the past for comfort.

"He was eternally youthful," Sanger says. "There was some reminiscing, signs of growing older. But there was also a thread to his ongoing life — people he had to see, friends he had to do favors for. He enjoyed the simple things. We lived for about six weeks in Stow. We'd come into Boston and on the way stop off at a diner in Hudson. He'd sit there and talk baseball with people and get genuine pleasure doing it. These were just people in a diner in Hudson, Massachusetts.

"He was certainly concerned with his intellectual interests. He discussed words and their roots. This was a real abiding interest. He felt that English was the rich language that it is because of its dual root in Latin and Anglo-Saxon. He would trace the meaning of any word based on how it came into usage, what it was borrowed from, what combination of syllables the word was made up of.

"But his basic linguistic interest was how modern French evolved from medieval French. This was a transition in the thirteenth, fourteenth, and even fifteenth centuries. He would have liked to have done a scholarly work on that subject, which apparently has never been adequately described. He did research for it and he was qualified to do it. It was something that had been on the burner in his mind for some time. He spoke of it as something he would get to next winter or next spring. Yet, he never got around to it."

There were signs that Moe's free spirit was not without cost. Recalls Arthur Daley, "Moe once said to me, 'Arthur, Arthur, there should be someone to remember you after everything passes.' He talked beautifully of his brother and said he wished he had had children too."

The catcher cuddled Sayre Ross's young daughter, Nancy, in his arms and asked, "Nancy, do you have a grandfather?"

"No, Moe, I don't.

"Then let me be your grandfather, Nancy, I would like that," he said.

Former Harvard baseball captain Warren S. Berg, no relative to Moe, adds: "Moe would come to Gloucester and we'd walk the beach. He'd spend endless time with my children teaching them Latin. They would trace the roots of words and have a beautiful time doing it. They were delighted by him."

In the spring of 1972 Moe had a lovely day. He had found a rare medieval book on French in a New York bookstore, for which he paid one dollar. Returning to Newark he alighted from a bus near his home; two men followed him and tried to mug him in the darkness. Berg held firmly to his book, sustaining blows as he fought them off. He then entered a nearby store and its proprietor asked if he were all right. Looking at his literary treasure, Moe Berg said, "We're fine, we're fine. My friend is over one hundred years old."

Moe Berg died on May 30, 1972, in Clara Maas Hospital in Newark, where he had been taken after suffering injuries in a fall at home.

Minutes before he died he turned to a nurse and spoke his last words.

"How did the Mets do today?" he asked.

Dan Daniel, retired New York newspaperman who had written of Berg, was at Frank Campbell's Funeral Chapel in New York City, where Moe's body lay in a flag-covered casket, and gave his assessment: "Moe Berg was a gentleman. The complete gentleman. When I think of the play

A Man for All Seasons, I think of Moe Berg. And I say this despite the fact it was tough to get to know Moe Berg. It was very tough to get close to him."

Fred Cochrane recalls, "I looked at that flag-covered casket and I said to myself, 'There's a man who knew more about the war than any person living. He was probably one of the few people in life who accomplished more by staying in the background of things than in the mainstream. It's a terrible handicap not to unload.' "

Tributes and condolences came from all parts of the world for baseball's foremost man of distinction.

Newspapers everywhere carried accounts of Moe Berg's baseball years, his mystery, and his gift for languages.

Some newspapers said Moe Berg spoke eight languages. Some newspapers said he spoke ten languages, and some newspapers suggested he spoke sixteen languages.

Boston Globe columnist Harold Kaese wrote a tender farewell to his friend. The headline over Kaese's column read: "Goodbye, Moe Berg, in any language."

Index